The Sacred World of the Penitentes

THE SACRED WORLD OF THE

PENITEN†ES

ALBERTO LÓPEZ PULIDO

SMITHSONIAN INSTITUTION PRESS
WASHINGTON AND LONDON

Copy editor: Tom Ireland
Production editor: Robert A. Poarch
Designer: Amber Frid-Jimenez

Library of Congress Cataloging-in-Publication Data
López Pulido, Alberto
    The sacred world of the Penitentes / Alberto López Pulido.
        p.   cm.
    Includes bibliographical references and index.
    ISBN 1-56098-974-2 (alk. paper) — ISBN 1-56098-394-9
(pbk. : alk. paper)
    1. Hermanos Penitentes.   2. Hispanic American
Catholics—New Mexico.   3. New Mexico—Religious life
and customs.   I. Title.

BX3653.U6 P85 2000
267'.242789—dc21   00-026523

British Library Cataloguing-in-Publication Data available

Manufactured in the United States of America
07 06 05 04 03 02 01 00   5 4 3 2 1

∞ The paper used in this publication meets the minimum
requirements of the American National Standard for
Information Sciences—Permanence of Paper for Printed
Library Materials ANSI Z39.48-1984.

For permission to reproduce illustrations appearing in
this book, please correspond directly with the owners of the
works, as listed in the individual captions. The Smithsonian
Institution Press does not retain reproduction rights for these
illustrations individually or maintain a file of addresses for
photo sources.

Frontispiece: Penitente carving *Pillars of the Southwest Church*
by Juan Sandoval. Photo courtesy Valarie Cordaro.

To the memory of my *abuelas* Francisca and Jennie,
with whom this story begins;

For my *padres* Alberto and Velia,
who taught me the value of *educación;*

For Linda,
who taught me to love unconditionally;

To the memory of Julian Samora,
who shared his love for New Mexico with all of us.

Contents

Preface

Even if there are no people left, one must remember. One
must remember. One must remember.

—Taida Sánchez-García, "I Know I Lived Very Comfortably"

In a mysterious and very powerful way, the writing of this book represents a journey of both personal and collective discovery. It has enabled me to simultaneously begin the process of giving a voice to those who have been either historically or generationally silenced. Through the written word, I find myself on the path toward discovering what the New Mexican writer Sabine Ulibarrí describes as my personal and collective *intrahistory*.[1] As a part of my own personal *story,* I can begin to reclaim "a heritage that flows unknown from generation to generation that one carries in their blood." As I reflect upon all the people that have shared their lives and stories along the way, mine seems to have fallen in place.

It began during one of those many summers when we returned to see family in the burgeoning agricultural community of Oxnard, California, a family ritual organized and directed by my mother through her conviction that we return to this community for as long as her dad, *mi abuelito,* was alive. We had left Oxnard in 1966 and moved south to San Diego for work. These northern journeys of three or more hours always began at four, sometimes three in the morning. The dark and cold departures were justified by our guide, my father, as the best way to outsmart L.A. traffic.

The home of my Tío Pancho and Tía Güera was a familiar place to us in our visits to Oxnard. Among the intimate smells coming from the very large casseroles of *carnitas* and *mole,* the kitchen was always the gathering place where countless hours were spent observing and learning about *familia* as we ate quietly and listened attentively to the debates over family politics between my Tío Pancho and his sister Velia, my mother. With arms and legs crossed, leaning back against the green-tiled sink, my uncle moved only to accentuate his point. Food was constantly being prepared in my *tía*'s kitchen. My mother sat concentrating on her work, shredding beef or cutting vegetables, looking up only to flick her meat- or vegetable-covered hand at my uncle to express her disagreement. I looked forward to these masterful debates because they taught me a great deal about family and ancestry.

It was during one of these many visits that I first saw the picture. It had to be sometime between the late seventies or early eighties because I was either an undergraduate at the University of California at San Diego (UCSD) or about to embark into graduate studies at the University of Notre Dame. To make his point in the midst of a friendly debate with my mother, my *tío* instructed my cousin to go get the picture. She returned with a shiny, square block of wood and placed it on the table. On the front, varnished onto the wood, was a picture of a young woman with a little boy on her lap. I had no idea as to who these people were, but the woman in the picture looked very much like my mother. As the debate resumed, I leaned over the table to get a better look at the picture and asked those around me to identify the two individuals. My uncle directed his attention to me, extended his arm, pointed at the photograph, and said, "That is me and my mother, that is your grandmother."

This came as a shock to me. I had always been told that María, my grandfather's second wife, was my maternal grandmother. The name Jennie came up every once in a while, but I had no clue about her place in the labyrinth of my ancestry. I know that my mother truly meant no harm by keeping this family secret. It was simply a way to keep the family together.

Juana (Jennie) Clare Amador was born in 1912 in Morenci, Arizona. She is my grandmother. Her mother, my great-grandmother, Francisca García Amador, was born in Ratón, New Mexico. From Arizona, they moved to California during the 1920s, where Jennie met a Mexican immigrant by the name of Antonio B. López in Oxnard. They were married in 1929 and lived and worked at La Limonera del Mar, a lemon orchard in nearby Santa Paula, California. Very little is known about the stories of either Francisca or Jennie, who died in April 1938 at the young age of twenty-six. As a result, her life, her story, and her death have been shrouded in mystery and silence for as long as I can remember.

Jennie was the descendant of an "illegitimate" union between her mother, Francisca, and a man named Clare in Arizona. One year prior to her death, Jennie was admitted into the Camarillo State Hospital for the mentally ill. According to her death certificate, she died of pneumonia and "exhaustion from manic psychosis." The silence, the unspoken words surrounding her birth and death, continue to trouble and haunt members of the family, including me. The loss of my *abuela,* Juana Amador, extinguished my New Mexican ancestry. The knowledge of it had been asleep inside of me, but this began to change when I saw the picture.

A year or two after the discovery and acknowledgment of the existence of Jennie Amador López, I was admitted into the Mexican American Graduate Studies Program at the University of Notre Dame to work under the direction of Julian Samora in the early eighties. The origins and lived expressions of the multifaceted Chicano community was something that fascinated me, and something I wanted to continually learn more about after I entered UCSD.[2] This desire, I realized, could only be fulfilled through advanced postbaccalaureate studies. The story around UCSD was that Dr. Samora supported graduate work in Chicano studies, something that I was unable to find anywhere else in the nation. Aside from this, I knew virtually nothing about the life and story of Professor Samora, just as I had known nothing about my grandmother. A pencil-sketched picture of him in a source book of famous Mexican Americans was my only source of information about this man.[3] Interestingly enough, the book had been a gift from my activist and unorthodox Tío Armando, who had served as a guide to me on a variety of issues related to the Chicano community and the contemporary Chicano movement ever since I was very young. I could feel that the tattered book, at one point in time in the life of my uncle, had been a testimony of pride and inspiration for young urban Chicanos wishing to transform society. But it had served its purpose, and it was time for him to pass it on.

In the years I spent in graduate studies at Notre Dame, I came to respect and admire the numerous achievements and accomplishments of Julian Samora as a precursor and pioneer of Chicano studies. As the first Mexican American sociologist in the history of this country, he personally mentored hundreds of students in the fields of sociology, history, political science, English, and law. Through his perspectives and *consejos,* I came to discover and understand the great love that Professor Samora had for his *tierra sagrada* of southern Colorado and northern Mexico. Born in Pagosa Springs, Colorado, he never ceased to instill in each of his students the legacy and strength of his land and of his people. As a result, the sacred connection to my New Mexican heritage, which for so long had been in abeyance, began to awaken inside of me, and I began to slowly name and embrace it as a part of my own personal sacred story.

It was during one of our many early morning meetings in Dr. Samora's library office, when we were discussing potential research topics, that he suggested that I examine the role of religion in the Chicano community. He felt strongly that this was going to become an important topic in the future, and one that Chicano/Latino scholars had mistakenly deemed irrelevant for scholarly study and analysis. In his typical unemotional, stoic way, he asserted that I could do "a hell of a job" if I chose to pursue this area of study. This is how I came to study the role of the sacred in the Chicano community, and eventually, to tell the story of the Hermanos Penitentes of New Mexico.

The guiding and organizing principle of this study is to tell the story of the penitente brotherhood. Story and storytelling represent the methodological approach that informs its perspective and theory. It is through story and storytelling that we organize *experiences* and endow them with meaning.[4] As one of our most important forms of cultural expression, stories allow us to capture the concrete particularities of past and present experiences because they tell us where people came from and where they are going.[5]

The experiences, traditions, and interpretations of a group are embodied in story. As several scholars have acknowledged, stories are symbolic "dwelling places"[6] that people live in, that provide us with "all the flesh and all the meaning"[7] of the whole or total experience.[8] Accordingly, this study examines and documents the stories that serve to mold and structure the history and sacred identity of the penitente community in New Mexico. These stories are placed with a specific social-historical and geographical space and context, which also enter into the shaping of penitente identity.[9]

This book represents a new and different story about the penitente brotherhood because it focuses on penitente understanding of and thinking about the sacred in their lives. It emphasizes the spiritual and religious character of the penitentes, which is at the root of this historic group. The sacred stories of the brotherhood orient the individual and collective experiences of people over time in relation to the "great powers" that establish reality and meaning in the penitente world.[10] It is through story that communities come to understand and interpret the "trail of legends" that encircles these great powers or deities with the exemplary behavior and character that guide communities.[11]

The community of La Fraternidad Piadosa de Nuestro Padre Jesús Nazareno, more commonly known as Los Hermanos Penitentes, has been a part of the New Mexican Hispano experience for centuries.[12] The story of La Hermandad, as it is also known, is best recounted as that of an important religious group that was credited with preserving the sacred traditions of northern New Mexico and southern Colorado as early as the eighteenth century. Current estimates place the Hermandad at six to seven hundred members within forty communities in the state of New Mexico.[13] Through acts of *caridad* (charity), *oración* (prayer), and *el buen ejemplo* (the good example), the brotherhood has been a guide and testament to Hispano Christianity that has maintained and supported unified communities throughout New Mexican history.

With historical and cultural roots in New Mexico, the stories of my *abuela* and of the penitente brotherhood are remarkably similar. Silence has defiled both of their stories. The silence that my grandmother's memory has endured is of the same type that the penitentes have withstood since the development of the American Southwest. Their contributions to the religious landscape of North America have been all but ignored and consequently marginalized by historians and storytellers of the American Southwest. We know very little about the sacred world of the penitentes, yet a great deal is known about the strange and deviant "cult," obsessed with self-flagellation, identified and defined as penitentes by the majority of scholars and storytellers of the Southwest. The marginalization through silence imposed upon the lives and stories of the brotherhood, like that imposed on my grandmother, has enabled others to distort and describe them as "crazy" because, as Maxine Hong Kingston reminds us, "insane people are those who cannot explain themselves."[14]

Marginal communities are bequeathed only a few fragments of their histories. Garrett Hongo tells us: "There are too many secrets and occlusions, too many reasons to forget the past. And there are forces which do not want us to remember, do not want us to take those fragments and complete them, to restore them to some fuller life. In the mainstream culture, in the popular media, in our educational systems, the stories and histories of people of color are deemed irrelevant at best, for the most part they do not exist, they've been wiped away."[15]

I wish to challenge the old story and offer a new one about the penitentes—a story that challenges the silences and distortions that have plagued the Hermandad. To challenge what one *hermano* clearly articulated when I first began this project: "las puras mentiras" (the pure lies) written about the Hermandad. In their place, I wish to overlay the unheard voices and expressions of the brotherhood that distinguishes it as an important sacred community. The writing of this book is a testament to the sacred memories, stories, and expressions of individuals, families, and communities who produced and sustained living and vibrant religious communities in New Mexico.

Acknowledgments

The initial work for this book began in the summer of 1992 when Padre Juan Romero introduced me to a host of individuals and communities throughout New Mexico. I thank this scholar of Padre Martínez, New Mexico's most famous priest, for his guidance in helping me initiate this project and for his continuing advice and words of encouragement. Since that time, I have examined and expanded the ideas of this work within numerous communities, where people have taken the time to share their insights and stories.

When this project began, I was on the faculty at the University of Utah, where several faculty and community members offered guidance. I wish to thank Archie Archuleta, Ronald Coleman, John Collette, Eduardo Elías, Jeff Garcilazo, Dair Gillespie, the late Clark Knowlton, Orlando Romero, Armando Solórzano, and Robert Velásquez.

In 1993 I began a new job at Arizona State University West. ASU has become an extremely supportive environment for me. Several colleagues have coalesced into a scholar's group known as Los Académicos Jodidos and provided invaluable insight into my work. I sincerely thank my fellow A.J.s: Sara Alemán, Celia Álvarez, Manuel Avalos, Gloria Cuádraz, Shari Collins Chobanian, Alejendra Elenes, and our inspiring leader, Mildred García. I appreciate all of your knowledge and expertise. I also thank Dan Arreola, Rose Díaz, Gary Keller, Anthony Hernández, Richard Lerman, Christine Marín, José Náñez, José Muñoz, and Santos Vega. All my colleagues in American Studies deserve special mention, in particular, the support offered by Dottie Broaddus, Joseph Comprone, and John Corrigan. A special word of thanks goes out to all past and present administrative assistants in our college, in particular, Dodie Peart and Beatrice Garvin.

A critical phase of this book was written during the 1995–96 academic year, when I was a visiting research scholar at the Center for Chicano Studies and the Department of Religious Studies at the University of California, Santa Barbara. The words and advice of several individuals were critical in moving this project forward. I wish to thank Alma Rosa Álvarez, Gretchen Bataille, Gastón Espinoza, Mario García, Richard Hecht, Luis Leal, Luis León, Charles Long, Ellen McCracken, Pat Richardson, Chela Sandoval, and Denise Segura.

The research for this book could have never been completed without the insight and guidance of archivists and librarians who were always there to serve. I wish to thank everyone at the New Mexico State Records Center and Archives, in particular, Sandra Jaramillo, Al Regensberg, Richard Salazar, and Robert Torrez. The guidance of Carolyn Atkins and the numerous volunteers at Menaul Historical Library of the Southwest were also invaluable. Marina Ochoa, archivist for the Archdiocese of Santa Fe, offered important advice and guidance. The library staff at Fletcher Library at Arizona State University West deserves a special thanks for all of the work they did for me. I wish to especially recognize deg farrelly, Dennis Isbell, Lisa Kammerlocher, and Donna Rodgers. Thank you for all of your patience and expertise.

I thank all of my students over the years, who have inspired me along the way. Special recognition goes out to Rebekah Barela, Héctor Borboa, Steve Miranda, Joseph Morales, and Jean Reynolds, who worked as research assistants on this book. I wish them the best in their careers.

Two scholarly organizations were instrumental in helping me develop my ideas for this work through academic conferences and informal gatherings. I wish to thank the National Association for Ethnic Studies, in particular, Susan Rockwell, Otis Scott, and Jesse Vazquez. I also wish to recognize the North American chapter of the Commission for the Study of History of Churches in Latin America (CEHILA), especially Gilbert Hinojosa, Timothy Matovina, Bishop Ricardo Ramírez, Moises Sandoval, and Robert Wright.

Financial support for this project came from numerous organizations. I thank the Center for Chicano Studies at the University of California, Santa Barbara; the College Summer Research Program at the University of Utah; the Cushwa Center for the Study of American Catholicism at Notre Dame; the Louisville Institute; and the Scholarship, Research, and Creative Activities Grant Program at Arizona State University West.

Numerous individuals deserve a special mention of thanks for all their friendship and scholarly expertise over the years. Jorge Huerta and Carlos Waisman were two professors who believed in me and supported me as an undergraduate at UCSD. Fabio Dasilva, Fred Wright, and the late Julian Samora served as mentors during my graduate career at Notre Dame. Fabio taught me to think, Fred taught me to teach, and Julian taught me to believe. I also thank the classmates who influenced me, especially Valarie Castillo, Paul López, and Arturo Zendejas.

David Abalos is one of my best friends and has guided me over the years on the journey of transformation that has profoundly impacted my personal and professional life. Otto Maduro has believed in my work from the very beginning and played a key role in helping me get some of my first publications. Miguel Carranza has supported me ever since I was a graduate student. Davíd Carrasco has always been an inspiration and mentor to La Chicanada from the first time I met him. He was instrumental in helping formulate several of the ideas in this book, and for that I truly thank him. Jennifer Pierce has been a wonderful friend and colleague over the years. Gilbert Cadena, Virgilo Elizondo, Lara Medina, and the late Antonio Soto asked important questions about the sacred world of Chicanos before anyone, and I thank them for all their work and insights. I wish to thank the Smithsonian Institution Press for supporting and believing in this project, especially Peter Cannell, Tom Ireland, Bob Lockhart, Scott Mahler, and Robert Poarch.

I thank my family: my parents, Velia and Alberto; my sister, Isabel; and my brother, José. You have always been there for me, and I love you. I also recognize Albertito, David, Esther, Gabriel, Gloria, Jenny, Laura, Marcus, Matthew, Oscar, Sergio, Robert, Robert Jr., Sara, Sergio, Timmy, and Wences. My *compa* Ray and my Tíos Armando and Pancho deserve special recognition for their friendship and support over the years. The late Antonio B. López, my grandfather, was an inspiration through his hard work and emotional love. My friend and wife, Linda Martínez Pulido, has believed in me from the first time we met. Thank you for all your support.

Numerous *manitas* and *manitos* have taken the time to carefully share their *cuentos, experiencias,* and expertise with me: Sister Emilia Atencio, Pauline Chávez Bent, Benito Córdova, Aurelio and Fructosa López, Amelia Maestas, Father Jerome Martínez y Alire, Lorraine Martínez, Felipe Mirabal, Candy and Luis Montoya, José Montoya, Michael Miller, Rev. Epifano Romero, Carmelita Romero, Susie Romero, Carmen Romero Velarde, and Leroy Vigil—friends, family, and members of the penitente brotherhood. I thank you all for sharing your hearts and minds with me. Finally, a special recognition goes out to Hermano Juan Sandoval, who through his advice and stories helped guide this project to completion. Through his example, he has taught me the Christian virtues of living a life of charity and prayer. For this, I am eternally grateful.

Introduction

The Importance
of the Story

Without that story, we grew up cipherously as if everything behind us was a zero and we were the first. To be
without history, to be without an emotional life, to be
without the ability even to imagine the emotional lives of
the people who came before you, is an incredibly damag-
ing thing, an ache that hurts in a way that you don't even
realize hurts.

—Garrett Hongo, *Under Western Eyes: Personal Essays from*
Asian America

The wander-thirst is like the drug-habit. Once you acquire
it you are done for. It will never let you rest. . . . It is as persistent as it is insidious. There comes the stage when you
think that you are cured of it. . . . But one day you casually
pick up a list of steamer sailings or stumble on your bat-
tered luggage plastered over with foreign labels, or whiff
some exotic smell which brings back memories of the hot
lands, or see a vessel outward bound, or idly open a map,
whereupon the old craving suddenly grips you like an
African fever, and almost before you realize it, you are on
the out-trail once again.

—E. Alexander Powell, *In Barbary: Tunisia, Algeria, Morocco and*
the Sahara

Carl N. Taylor was born in 1903 in the town of Milltown, Indiana. A professional writer with degrees in English from Central Normal College and the University of New Mexico, he told stories for a living. His many accounts about Asia and the Philippines came from his colorful life as a traveler, vagabond, and adventurer in search of the "uncivilized" and "wild" parts of the world.

His vagabond spirit brought him great recognition with the publication of his book *Odyssey of the Island*,[1] where through story he recounts his adventures while "tramping" through "partially civilized" portions of the Philippines. His book was well received as "a straightforward human narrative of observation and discovery among little known peoples."[2] It was described as "an exciting record of adventure, of peril from wild people, wild animals and the most constant menace of all from the vagaries of a wild land and a wild sea."[3]

As a self-described "writer of travel," Taylor returned to the United States in the fall of 1935 looking forward to the familiar challenge of composing yet another story of adventure for his reading public. He situated himself in a mountain cabin in the Sandia Mountains, twenty-five miles east of Albuquerque, New Mexico, in the community of Cedar Crest. With assistance from Roy De S. Horn, his publisher and literary agent, Taylor was soon at work on a piece for *Today* magazine. His assignment: to construct and tell the story of the brothers of Nuestro Padre Jesús El Nazareno, more commonly known as Los Hermanos Penitentes of New Mexico.

By the winter of 1936, Taylor had completed his penitente story, *Agony in New Mexico,* and sent it off for publication. On the evening of February 5, he chose to relax after dinner with a copy of *In Barbary,* written by one of his favorite authors, Alexander E. Powell. Taylor was a great admirer of Powell, whose "flair for adventure" was similar to his own.[4]

At around 8:00 P.M. that evening, the local justice of the peace, Faustino Chávez, came face to face with a distraught Modesto Trujillo, who appeared at Chávez's home near the Taylor cabin. Trujillo informed Chávez that there was trouble at the Taylor place. Upon arriving at the cabin, Chávez and Trujillo discovered Carl Taylor lying face down in a pool of blood, in the living room of the cabin. He had been shot to death.

A young man of nearly sixteen, Trujillo had been employed by Taylor as a "houseboy" to perform a variety of domestic chores. He was taken to Albuquerque for questioning by the authorities, and later that evening, he confessed to the murder of Carl Taylor. According to District Attorney Thomas J. Mabry, robbery was the sole motive for the killing, and all other theories had been discarded.[5] On February 17, nearly two weeks after the murder, the young Trujillo entered a plea of guilty to second-degree murder. He was sentenced by Judge Fred E. Wilson to serve ninety-nine to one hundred years in the state penitentiary.

In *Agony in New Mexico,* Carl Taylor describes most Cedar Crest residents as honest, simple, and cheerful, with a highly developed sense of community obligation toward their neighbors, people who never hesitated to assist with the hungry, the ill, the newborn, and the deceased.[6] Yet, as in the tradition of other "vagabond narratives" about New Mexico, Taylor had inevitably "discovered" the "grim" and "beastly" act of self-flagellation and the whish! thud! of the penitential whips.[7] According to his narrative, he had witnessed a crucifixion unfold right before his eyes, performed by voting citizens of the Republic.[8]

These self-defined "vagabond narratives" are stories of exploration that seek to document eyewitness accounts of the exotic anomalies, wonders, and scandals of newly discovered worlds. They are imagined and constructed from the storytellers' encounter with "unfamiliar data"; they claim their validity by making constant references to actual experiences.[9] All of these stories describe a people who look, speak, and act differently from those who tell the story. The storytellers are mostly travelers who find the topography and landscape of the Southwest strange and unfamiliar, which helps explain the "unique" phenotype, language, and behavior of these newly discovered people and their region.

Vagabond writer murdered among the penitents: what a story! Roy De S. Horn and Raymond Moley, editors of *Today* magazine, believed a plot was behind the killing, and they were in a prime position to have their voices heard. They were convinced that Taylor was murdered as a result of his not-yet published exposé.[10] The Taylor murder drew immediate national attention, for it was the kind of stuff that sold newspapers and packed people in at the local movie house.[11] Although none of the allegations put forth by Horn or Moley were ever substantiated, the Taylor murder was clearly the one defining story that introduced and interpreted the penitentes to mainstream America in the twentieth century.[12]

Stories by and about Carl Taylor embody part of a master narrative by the rough-and-tough individuals who historically risked their lives for the sake of uncovering the "barbaric" and "heathenistic" practices of people who lived in some remote village in the American Southwest, beginning with the United States occupation in the mid-nineteenth century. These stories offer an explanatory framework for understanding all historical events and constructs related to penitente identity and expressions in the history of the Southwest. The most typical penitente accounts, for as long as writers, photographers, artists, and academics have labored to preserve them, are stories of danger and adventure told from the perspective of the vagabond or outsider.[13]

Consequently, the hundreds of accounts that claim to capture the sacred qualities of the brotherhood fail to appreciate the presence of the sacred in the everyday life experiences of the people. They ignore the fact that the sacred is at the core of penitente identity, experiences, and expressions. Instead, these writers are drawn to the outlandish and exotic contours of the penitente community. Most previous works attempt, at best, to tell the penitente story through documentation of Holy Week rites and ritual in the Christian calendar. As a result, the penitente experience is essentially silenced, restricted to a narrow and often incorrect interpretation of the sacred in the lives of the people and community. In fact, most penitente accounts are driven solely by the desire to *desacral-*

An example of the type of newspaper article that appeared soon after the Carl Taylor murder. Reprinted with permission from the *Cleveland Plain Dealer,* copyright 1936, all rights reserved.

ize the community by exposing the "profane" actions and expressions of this so-called sacrilegious community in an attempt to expose the wrongful ways of the brotherhood.

For such storytellers, the historical and contemporary penitentes represent the antithesis to the sacred. As with other aspects of Hispano and Chicano history in the Southwest, the penitente brotherhood has been shrouded with inaccurate historical images that need to be redressed and interpreted from the perspective of the people who form part of this religious group.

This book offers a different penitente story. It builds and creates a story with the living experiences, expressions, and utterances of the Hermandad as a foundation in order to chronicle the penitentes' sacred story and legacy from their own perspective. As a result, this work explores and explains two essential questions: What is it that makes a penitente story sacred? How do these stories work to *sacralize* the Hispano community and its history? Therefore, the focus of this book is first, to understand what the belief in Nuestro Padre Jesús El Nazareno (Our Father Jesus the Nazarene) represents to a penitente, and second, how this belief shapes human agency and transforms their world into a sacred place.

Unlike past penitente studies, such as Marta Weigle's landmark book, *Brothers of Light, Brothers of Blood,* this book will not offer a descriptive account of penitente rites and rituals.[14] Instead, it focuses on the *meaning* of the sacred in the lives of the brothers, as told through story, in an attempt to capture those sacred symbols that are an integral part of their sacred world. The penitente story told in this book is of a people for whom the sacred has always been an intimate and indispensable part of their lives—a story in which the role of the sacred is taken very seriously. The words of stories and their meanings, in relation to the great powers that establish penitente reality, are understood in this work to be sacred.[15]

In this study, a sacred story also represents a *lyric* with spiritual qualities that orient us toward those things that are real and meaningful in our lives.[16] Stories serve as concrete and literal guides, like art or performance, that are enacted in our quest for understanding and knowing the sacred. The lyrics of the stories are presented here by documenting spoken language, which unlocks the archaic patterns of spiritual creativity and guides communities.[17] It is through story that I will strive to uncover and interpret the lyrics of penitente and Hispano spirituality.

This work is guided by a theoretical and methodological framework that embraces the belief that people construct and create culture through the telling of their own story. Penitente stories emerge out of a people's experiences, expressions, motivations, intentions, and actions.[18] Story provides a space where people share in the sacred perspective or vision of a particular individual and of his or her community. We discover the layers of a people's history and their myths by knowing their story.[19] Story and storytelling represent the central methodological tool for understanding and interpreting the presence of the sacred in the everyday life experiences and expressions of the penitente brotherhood.

The significance and focus of story and storytelling in this research lie directly in the actions of people and their roots in social and cultural life.[20] In this study, for example, we will discover a Hispano penitente sacred tradition shaped by a style of Christianity firmly rooted in the experiential and practical dimensions of human agency. As a result, we pay close attention to those individual, social, historical, economic, political, and cultural factors that shape and give meaning to a story in the context of the everyday life experiences and expressions of the brotherhood.

Chapter 1 introduces the sacred world of the penitentes. A complete overview and examination of the Carl Taylor murder is presented in chapter 2, and in chapter 3, the master narrative of that event is juxtaposed to the penitente sacred narrative. In chapter 4 I interpret the penitente sacred triad of charity, prayer, and the good example within the context of a sacred expression defined as *practical Christianity*. The fifth chapter reviews the emerging discipline of Hispano/Chicano religions.[21] I argue for the incorporation of story and storytelling as a method of understanding and interpreting manifestations of the sacred in the Hispano/Chicano experience.

This book is based on archival research, fieldwork, and interviews in northern New Mexico and Albuquerque, New Mexico, beginning in 1992. The original and new research for this book comes from numerous discussions and interviews with *hermanos,* and the relatives of *hermanos,* compiled over the past seven years. However, the most important and significant contribution to this research project comes from one *hermano mayor* (elder) with whom I have spoken continually about penitente sacred experiences since 1992.[22]

Haciendo Penitencia

Caridad, Oración, y el Buen Ejemplo

> El penitente es una persona que hace penitencia.
>
> (A penitent is one who does penance.)
>
> —A penitente brother

Throughout various communities in New Mexico, one often hears the story about the widow or orphan who, due to the loss of family, find themselves in need of material aid and support. In the story, the plight of the widow or orphan is resolved by members of the community who respond expeditiously to the needs of the less fortunate. Candy Martínez, for example, who grew up in Truchas, New Mexico, has fond memories of "las tradiciones de antes" (past traditions). She remembers it as a place where there was always community among the people: "Siempre había comunidad" (There was always community), she recalls. "My dad owned a ranch, and all of my uncles and the neighbors always came to help him. They would cut and bundle the wheat; we would make dinner, and everyone would eat and share. When the other people had work, then we in turn would go and help them."[1] She asserts, "If something ever happened; if any of the people were going through any type of *tribulación* [affliction], then the other families were ready to assist them, be it with food, or with any other type of aid, but the families were always united."[2] Her narrative is part of a larger collective history that, over the centuries, has taught the values of mutuality, reciprocity, and self-determination in the New Mexican region.[3]

Layered deeply within these teachings are the sacred experiences and expressions of the penitente brotherhood. According to penitente oral teachings, to help a widow or orphan is to partake in *una obra de caridad* (an act of charity). We are told: "Over the years, the brothers *accarrearon* [gathered] these communities with much pride, but without self-aggrandizement, for it was simply a part of their teachings. They helped sustain the homes and harvest the lands of those that needed help—the widows, the orphans. They provided succor by means of prayer and spiritual exercises in the *moradas* [sacred abodes]. [The brothers] could gather the community because in those days, everyone was united and knew where to go for prayer, spiritual, and personal help."[4]

An act of charity, the most important sacred expression by the Hermandad, is achieved through *oración* (prayer) and *el buen ejemplo* (the good example). Acts of charity, prayer, and the good example are at the core of the penitente sacred experience.

The Story of *Caridad* in Penitente History

The history of Christianity in New Mexico is predominantly the story of Roman Catholicism in the Americas as it traversed geographical regions from south to north. Consequently, it is best characterized as a ubiquitous religious tradition that is impossible to contain within the institutionalized boundaries of American Roman Catholicism. From the first settlements until at least territorial time, the New Mexican region had no resident bishop or seminary and suffered from a chronic shortage of priests.[5] New Mexico was perceived as isolated and dangerous, with few if any rewards for those who settled there, and it was avoided by Catholic clergy. By 1830, close to half of the 4,299 prelates who had entered the Mexican frontier, the majority of whom were Spanish, had departed.[6] In a historically isolated territory with little support or direction from a religious clergy, New Mexican Catholics produced a unique type of Catholicism that was self-reliant and laity-centered.[7] As a result, the sacred emerged within a unique political, economic, social, and cultural context that was intertwined with the personal, everyday life experiences and expressions of a people. The local faith that evolved represents a resilient people characterized as rural, communal, self-determined, and devout. From within this history and tradition emerged Los Hermanos Penitentes.

The penitentes are directly credited with preserving sacred traditions in a region bereft of the official Catholic sacraments and other priestly ministrations central to the tenets of Roman Catholicism. The Hermandad emerged as a civil and ecclesiastical organization, leading the community in prayer, worship, and catechism. At the same time, the brotherhood made sure everyone had the basics for a sufficient quality of life through collective irrigation and harvesting of the lands.[8] At the core of this belief system was charity *(caridad)*, the means of understanding and living in the world.

Members of the Hermandad credit charitable works with having gathered and sustained New Mexican communities over the centuries. Charity has been a way to vigilantly "look out" for those in the community in need of help. The people have always known where to go for spiritual help. "Iban para las moradas porque no había clero católico" (They would go to the moradas because there was no Catholic clergy).[9] The brotherhood succored the community through prayer, which was directly linked to acts of charity. Praying and providing help to those in need are understood as synonymous sacred acts. One penitente regards his childhood as a "complete act of charity," a life in which people in the community were always seeking to help one another. "When we finished harvesting our land, it was automatic for us to go with the neighbor and help them with theirs."[10] Throughout the history of the Southwest, and in particular New Mexico and southern Colorado, the Hermandad continued to maintain their belief in charity and benevolence through their sustained actions of helping members of the community, as they do today.

Prayer as Penance: Charity, Prayer, the Good Example

To act toward one another with charity and mutual love like brothers in
Jesus Christ; to provide a good example for each other, helping in illness,
afflictions, and time of need . . .

—Oath of the Taos Cofradía, 1861, from "Community Functions of the Cofradía de
Nuestro Padre Jesús Nazareno," by Paul Kutsche and Dennis Gallegos

The most salient characteristic that defines a penitente is the practice of
penitencia (penance). This act of penance is experienced and expressed
through manifestations and oral teachings of charity that inspire and
guide spiritual and material activity for the brotherhood and for the community at large.[11] From this perspective, it is understood that charity is
a penitential act, and that to be a penitente, one must strive to practice
acts of charity.

Charity is described as an act of penance because "requiere que tengo
que salirme de mi camino" (it requires me to go out of my way) for the
sake of *haciendo oración* (doing prayer) for someone or the community
at large.[12] It represents an act of charity, an act one ordinarily does not
have to do, but which, in the doing, it is transformed into an act of
penance. One sacred story that defines and sustains *caridad* in the penitente world is that of Valerosa Verónica.

The Via Crucis (Way of the Cross) is a pilgrimage devotion experienced by the penitente brotherhood to accompany Jesus in his passion.
As a devotion that was disseminated throughout the world by the Franciscan Order, the Via Crucis plays a prominent role in Semana Santa
(Holy Week) observances for penitentes. The passion of Jesus represents
a plan for how one should live one's daily life: "The most important thing
to understand regarding the passion of the Lord is that every step that He
took was in order to give us an example with His life on how we are sup-
pose to live."[13]

The Stations of the Cross are said to have been originated in the twelfth
and thirteenth centuries by veterans of the Crusades who erected tableaux

in their homes representing various places they had visited in the Holy Land. The custom was borrowed by the Franciscans, who eventually brought the practice to the Americas. Historically, the number of stations varied from as few as five to over thirty, until in 1731, Pope Clement XII routinized them at fourteen.[14] It is at stations number five and six where we learn the story of Valerosa Verónica. The penitente narrative of Valerosa Verónica is as follows:

> La historia que se ha dicho y las tradiciones que tenemos nosotros sucedió en la estación cinco pero la nombran número seis. Por que allí estaba una piedra que hasta el día de hoy se enseña en Jerusalem y allí se sentó el Señor mientras que allaba quien le ayudara con la cruz. Y en eso se vino una mujer: Valerosa Verónica y se vino por entre toda la gente sin que nadie la molestara con el valor de ir a limpiar el rostro al Señor.

> The story that is told and that is a part of our traditions occurred at station number five but is referred to as number six. It is said that there was a rock at this location that till this day is still shown in Jerusalem where the Lord sat while they found someone who could help him carry the cross. During this process, Courageous Veronica came forth from among the people and dared to wipe the face of our Lord, and no one bothered her. (translation by author)

The penitente story of the passion of Jesus tells us that He sat on a rock waiting while soldiers tried to find someone who would help Him carry the cross. "No one was willing to come forward to help Him because according to the law, he who carried the cross would die upon it."[15] Frustrated by their inability to find anyone, the penitente narrative says, the soldiers were forced to hire Simon of Cyrene to help Jesus carry the cross. This event is officially recognized as the fifth station of the cross.

During this period of waiting, the penitente story relates, Valerosa Verónica came forward from among the people to wipe the face of Jesus with her veil. In response, the Lord rewarded her for her courageous act: her veil was left marked with the image of Jesus' face. Penitentes officially recognize the actions by Valerosa Verónica as the sixth station of the cross but are cognizant that it may have occurred during the fifth station.

In addition, a person *hace caridad* (accomplishes acts of charity) through the act of *haciendo oración*. Charity represents the spiritual pursuit, as praying represents the way to realize this spiritual objective. For penitentes, acts of charity are tantamount to prayer, and in that respect both are acts of penance.

More importantly, prayer is talked about and understood in a very different way from traditional prayer within the penitente sacred tradition. To state that you are *haciendo oración* means that you are *literally* doing prayer or praying. "We attempt to emulate the life of Christ, not just by words but through our actions," attests one brother.[16] Prayer is understood as an act or performance by a group or individual and an integral part of penitente history and traditions. This approach moves us beyond those perspectives that examine prayer largely in the analysis of written text, where prayer is described as a formulaic, redundant, and trite verbal act. Instead, prayer as practiced by the penitentes needs to be seen as a spontaneous creative act, constructed by a performance that includes a wide religious and cultural context in association with the words.[17] Therefore, doing prayer or praying means prayer as agency: "Prayer does not mean that I am going to kneel and pray. Prayer can also mean that I am going to see what it is that those people *[aquella gente]* needs are and then I am going to help them."[18]

Finally, prayer as agency is creatively identified as *el buen ejemplo de oración* (the good example of prayer). This means that by praying (meaning prayer that produces acts of charity), one provides a good example to the brotherhood and the community at large. *El buen ejemplo* (the good example) is accomplished by charitable acts with or without personal prayer. *El buen ejemplo* without personal prayer is accomplished by charitable or merciful acts that are synonymous with prayer. It represents one of the most important values within the penitente tradition: "For my Fa-

Santa Verónica holding the veil. She is recognized in the penitente community as Valerosa Verónica. School of José Aragón, 1820–40. Photo courtesy Taylor Museum, Colorado Springs Fine Arts Center.

ther God prefers the good example that you do with your life rather than if you are praying. Pray all day long but don't tell no one you understand? One goes with the other naturally."[19] *El buen ejemplo* with personal prayer means that you offer personal prayer for someone in addition to assisting or helping them. It consists of "asking my Father God through the medium of prayer that he succor a family that finds itself alone or forsaken, and in addition, one sees if this [person] needs wood or whatever. If so, one would collect it and bring it to them." In sum, one is told that in this life, no one "puede ganarle a la oración y el buen ejemplo" (can "beat out" praying and the good example) because only through them will one find *caridad*.[20]

The Story of Santiago Luna

> Mi Dios Y mi redentor
> en quien espero y confió
> Por tu pasión Jesús Mío
> abrasame en vuestro amor.
> —A popular and enduring *alabado* (hymn)

Hermano Santiago Luna is a devout follower and teacher of penitente sacred tradition throughout the state of New Mexico. He represents three generations of penitente tradition and experience: both his father and his grandfather were penitentes. Twenty-seven years ago, he experienced a religious conversion in his life and decided to join the penitente brotherhood. What follows is his life story. In his own words, it tells of how Hispano and penitente sacred traditions have molded and shaped his experience.[21]

> It was 1972, during La Cuaresma [Holy Week], on Good Friday, that I recall driving rather slowly and indecisively around the block several times in front and behind the *morada*, uncertain about my recent decision. A *morada* is a sacred abode where the brothers gather and meditate on the passion of our

Lord. Earlier that day, I had informed my wife that I was going to attend services at the one and only *morada* in Albuquerque, New Mexico.

My life had taken numerous turns, taking me and my family to various places, inside and outside the state of New Mexico. Yet, through it all, especially during the Lenten season, there were always those childhood memories of the countless penitente services that I attended as a young man that sustained me. The collective sounds of the powerful *alabados* [hymns] and *oraciones* [prayers] as performed by the *viejitos* [elders] inside the *morada* were always *within* me.

My plan on this day was to go and ask that I be accepted into the penitente brotherhood. However, after coming face to face with my decision, I was no longer certain that I wanted to go through with it. I knew *pa donde iba* [where I was going], and I didn't feel that I was man enough, you know. My indecisive thoughts were interrupted by an elderly man who came up to my car and rather directly asked, "Hey man, what are you looking for?" Somewhat embarrassed, I replied with a question of my own: "Is this where the *morada* is located?" "Yes," the elderly man responded, "there are brothers in there, park your car and go inside." Almost in tears, I entered, and was accepted into the Hermandad.

I was born in Los Ojitos, New Mexico, in 1934 at the tail end of the Depression. My parents along with several other family members had migrated from northern New Mexico and homesteaded in what became Los Ojitos. Los Ojitos was a settlement on the Pecos River at the head of Sumner Lake. My family experienced numerous hardships there because the land was arid, without water or even *pajaritos* [birds]. My family had discovered and eaten every single edible plant or vegetation that grew in the area such as *chimajá* [wild parsley] and *palmilla* [yucca] in order to survive. After spending five difficult years on the land, required of all homesteaders by the government, my parents became property owners and were now eligible to sell their property.

About a year after I was born, we sold our property and moved to Puerto de Luna, New Mexico, around twelve miles north of Los Ojitos.[22] For me,

Puerto de Luna was a glorious place. Along with my older brother Juan, we came to discover every inch of this beautiful gateway to the *llano* [plain]. It is true that we had to work every day of our lives in order to survive, but I have a lot of fond memories of growing up in Puerto de Luna. For us kids, the best part of the year were the months of April and May, when we plowed and planted during the day, but our evenings were free for us to go swimming in the river. All of us would gather to fish, play games, and feast on a chicken that we had taken from an unsuspecting neighbor on our way to the river.

Religion was a part of my daily life while growing up in Puerto de Luna. You had no choice in the matter, you either grew up in a religious home, or you were sent to catechism. In addition to praying the rosary nightly with family, a *viejita* by the name of Doña Petra served as my teacher of religion. Doña Petra, who was also my *madrina* [godmother], was teacher to all of the children who lived on this side of the river. She was a strict teacher who taught through memorization. My *madrina* taught us catechism, and she would pull our ears if we didn't memorize our lesson. Her main objective was to prepare us for our First Holy Communion as determined by the roaming Roman Catholic priest who visited the area periodically. Our Catholic faith was passed down through family and friends. The priest would visit the nearby *capilla* [chapel] of Nuestra Señora del Refugio by *carro de caballo* [horse and wagon] to offer a weekly Mass, attended faithfully by all of my family. I remember on Sundays awakening at five in the morning in order to hitch the mules to the family wagon and journey four miles to the chapel. Once Doña Petra felt that we, her catechism students, were ready, she would set a date with the priest, who, in turn, would test us on our Catholic knowledge by oral examination. If we passed, then he would give us our first communion.

The Hermanos Penitentes of my childhood in Puerto de Luna have made an everlasting impression on my life. I remember the people would walk four, five, or six miles to the *morada* because this is where the brothers prayed the Stations of the Cross. The brothers prayed their *alabados*, prais-

ing God, and praying the Stations of the Cross, and we would join them. The
rosaries and wakes were conducted by the brothers. I grew up, got married,
and all of that, but when Lent arrived, there were those *alabados* and
prayers inside of me—what I had heard! They were holy *alabados* that
spoke directly about the *pasión de Cristo* [passion of Christ]. I experienced
and truly understood what has become my most memorable *alabado,* which
claims: "My God and my redeemer in whom I hope and trust, through your
passion, my Jesus, embrace me with your love."[23]

These are the most unforgettable moments of my life, which are truly un-
explainable through words. It is easier for me to describe these memorable
sacred expressions as *sentimientos* [feelings] because I cannot put them
into words. In my mind, they are feelings that one must experience in order
to fully understand their significance. You understand this because I am
telling you what happened, *pero* [but] you don't really understand it because
you weren't there to experience it. I was there, and that experience has
stayed with me.

It was these experiences from the *morada* of my childhood that drew me
to the Albuquerque *morada* back in 1972. Unfortunately, it was sustained by
only a small group of elderly men, and the owner of the property decided to
shut it down that same year. Sadly enough, the one and only Albuquerque
morada where I became a penitente was closed at the end of the Lenten season in 1972. As I look back now I realize that it was all part of God's plan that
this happened. Because God led me to ask, how come in Albuquerque, the
biggest town in New Mexico, how come we don't have a *morada? Y allí
comencé mi pelea* [And this is when I began my fight]. My fight was to establish a *morada* in the city of Albuquerque because we didn't have one. But
it wasn't me, *era mi* Tata Dios (it was my Father God). This is why as a
young man I went over to the Albuquerque *morada* among those *viejitos,*
and this is why it was shut down. It *forced* me to start looking and searching
until God brought me here to my present-day *morada,* and I have been
grateful ever since. I have worked like an animal, me and my family, to have
this, but it doesn't matter, that has no bearing on it whatsoever.

So this same year, with assistance from friends and family, we began to restore an abandoned Roman Catholic church in Albuquerque that was over 245 years old. I remember, I would bring my wife to come look at the abandoned church, and she would just feel sorry for me because it was such a mess, but she couldn't see what I was seeing. Our very first task was to cut the two front wooden doors to the entrance of the *morada.* After fitting the doors, something inside of me said that these doors were incomplete. So I was moved to carve into the doors the image of San José on the left door, and an image of Nuestro Padre Jesús el Nazareno on the right. Since this time, several of us have been working steadily to refurbish both the interior and exterior sections of the *morada.* I repaired a collapsed wall within the sacristy that had to be reconstructed. The sanctuary was covered in soot due to extensive fire damage and had to be meticulously scrubbed, cleaned, and painted, and a section had to be rebuilt. The entire *morada* was reinforced and strengthened with new adobe, and the exterior surface was replastered. A *portal* [porch] at the entrance of the morada was designed and built, and a new roof was added. The list is endless.

Around 1985, I decided to design, construct, and erect life-size images of the Stations of the Cross made entirely out of cement. These were images created without molds and were all hand painted. They have been placed outside around the *morada* for Lenten observances. All of this marked the beginning of a new Albuquerque *morada* that was restored out of an abandoned church, *y gracias a mi* Tata Dios [and thanks to my Father God], it continues as one of the most active *moradas* in the state of New Mexico.

When I carved the doors for the entrance into the morada, it is important to understand, I had been carving for less than a year. When I think about it, carving has really changed my life. It all began through a coworker who, during his free time, was carving wood with a pocket knife. I was on vacation and had gone into work to pick up my paycheck. I had never seen him do that, and I was always wanting to do something on rock, that was my thing, but I had never done it. So I told him, when I return from my vacation I'm going to try something like that, and he told me, I'll show you how to use the knife. I went back and I started, and he never did it anymore, and I just kept on going.

During this same period of my life, I began searching for answers from my Tata Dios about my life, so I began to study and meditate heavily. I was studying the passion of our Lord *muy* [very] in depth, you know, because I wanted to know exactly where I was at. It was through my studies, meditations, and newly discovered gift of carving that it all came together for me. I said to myself, why don't I make the last twenty-three hours of Christ's life, you know, carve them, and that way I can share it with the Hermandad. I carved a total of thirty-eight "scenes" that mark the passion of our Lord, beginning on Holy Thursday through Good Friday, when Christ dies on the cross. Through my work, I meditate on the "price" that Christ paid for me.

What emerged out of all of this is what I describe as my vocation, which I share with the Hermandad and the community at large. I call it a vocation because it is directly related to the *sentimientos* associated with my experiences of being a penitente. In my opinion, this is what truly makes a penitente. It is a deep feeling inside oneself, where you have to feel the words and actions beyond just words. As they say in English, "It's in the blood," and basically, if it's not in the blood, then the words, prayers, or actions do not matter. Feelings and sentiments are required in being a penitente. Some brothers describe having *sentimientos de tristesa* [feelings of sorrow] after having recited certain prayers or *alabados,* but I experience *brincos de mi corazón* [my heart skipping a beat] as I am drawn closer to my Tata Dios through the experience. I now have a countless amount of carvings representing religious scenes that I use to educate the brotherhood and the community on the life, death, and resurrection of Jesus Christ. These teachings are what I refer to as *misiones* [missions], where, through my carvings, I teach the ways of Christ's passion and His love for us. I continue to offer these missions throughout the state of New Mexico, and I have carved and given a *bulto* [statue of a saint] to every *morada* in the state of New Mexico.

I want people to understand what one can do with their life if you give it over to your Tata Dios. To go *de la nada* [from nothing] to being a follower

of God as a penitente and a recognized teacher, this is what is important to
remember about my life. I really see the hand of God in my life![24] This is
how the brotherhood has changed my life.

The life story of Santiago Luna as a member of the penitente brotherhood illustrates how charity, prayer, and the good example remain an integral element in his personal and collective spiritual development. As a
person who was taught the sacred ways of the brotherhood through family and community teachings, Hermano Luna incessantly sought those
experiences and expressions that drew him closer to the sacred that was
so familiar to him.

In a region where resident clergy were visibly absent from the sacred
landscape, the idea of teaching and passing on the faith through family,
friends, and kin was common in the boldest and creative expressions re-
garded as Hispano popular Catholicism. Clearly, it was the role of clergy,
as "examiners," to affirm the presence of institutional religion in these
communities. But just as important, if not more so, the elders like Doña
Petra served as teachers of the community, infusing sacred and cultural
expressions into the lives and experiences of future generations. Such experiences and expressions represent part of a larger collective, economic,
political, and cultural history, and through extremely practical means,
have persistently taught the sacred values of mutuality, reciprocity, and
self-determination characteristic of Hispano and penitente identity.

These values are embedded in a sacred history guided by the values and
teachings of charity, prayer, and the good example. As an active member
of the penitente brotherhood, Hermano Luna seeks to enact and perform
acts of charity within his everyday life. Such charitable or merciful acts,
in themselves a kind of prayer, are good examples for the whole world
to witness. Such acts are grounded in the concrete material world within
everyday life experiences. They represent a very practical form of religiosity and Christianity, defined as practical Christianity.

This is Hermano Luna's *vocation* in life. As an Hermano Penitente, he sees his entire life as a vocation in which, through his carved works, he educates and teaches people about the Christian passion. Reflecting on how God has guided him into the brotherhood and endowed him with a gift for woodcarving, he reflects: "I was meant to be here. I LOVE IT! The passion of the Lord, *lo que El sufrió por mí* [what He suffered for me], I appreciate it! The price he had to pay for the redemption of my sins. I want the whole world to understand that, and I want the whole world to appreciate that too. Including the resurrection and everything else naturally, but basically the redemptive part of our blessed Lord is what moves me to pieces. *Aquí estoy!* [Here I am!]"[25]

As unique and individual sentiments, charity, prayer, and the good example must nevertheless be woven together to understand the meaning of *penitencia* and the key role of Christ's passion in penitente story and tradition. Furthermore, as paths toward Tata Dios or the sacred, *caridad, oración,* and *el buen ejemplo* require a real and active expression of the sacred, which is to say, all sacred acts represent overt and real manifestations of and about the sacred.

Risking It All
for Civilization

2

In the strange, marijuana-maddened minds of the Mexican
Indians who call themselves the Penitentes, they are
Brothers in the Blood of Christ. By their own blood,
by the agony of whips flaying their own naked flesh, they
re-enact again the crucifixion at Calvary and atone in
themselves for the agony of Christ.
—*Cleveland News,* February 8, 1936

I went the easy way, on improved highways, to the towns
of Chimayó, Truchas, Abiquiu, and Ranchitos. . . . Tourists
and Penitente-peepers were there in force. They came
with cameras, and they brought cigarettes to bribe the
Brothers Penitent. Around the tightly closed and strangely
quiet moradas they set up their tripods and waited, complaining that no real Penitente showed up to pose even for
a price. . . . A woman with a box camera clutched in her
gloved hands stopped me in Abiquiu. "When do things
start around here?" she wanted to know. "I expected to
see blood running in the street."
—Marcus Bach, *Faith and My Friends*

V agabond writer Carl Taylor was murdered on February 5, 1936, after completing his penitente story, *Agony in New Mexico*. A young man of nearly sixteen, Modesto Trujillo, confessed to the crime twelve days later and entered a guilty plea to second-degree murder. He was sentenced to ninety-nine to one hundred years in the state penitentiary. From a legal standpoint, it was an open-and-shut murder case with robbery as the motive. Yet the printed media, led by Roy De S. Horn, Taylor's literary agent, and Raymond Moley, editor of *Today* magazine, was not convinced that robbery was the sole motive behind the killing. Because it drew such diffused and exaggerated coverage, the story was primarily responsible for introducing and defining penitente identities and practices to mainstream America in the twentieth century. The master narrative or explanatory framework embodied in the Taylor story has its roots in the mid- to late nineteenth century through the first documented travel narratives of Josiah Gregg and Charles Lummis.

"Taylor may have been the victim in some strange penitente plot," stated Horn when asked by the Associated Press about the motive behind the killing.[1] Horn went on to state that he had recently received from Taylor three photographs of the interior of the penitente *morada* in Cedar Crest and claimed that these pictures "may have had some bearing on the slaying."[2] For Moley, a paragraph in Taylor's *Agony in New Mexico* was a clear indication that Trujillo was directly connected to the penitentes: "The boy who chops wood for me and who, I think, secretly cherishes an ambition some day to be elected the village *Cristo* and hang upon a cross, is immensely proud of his shiny new bicycle."

The media was convinced that Carl Taylor had been murdered in a penitente plot and that Trujillo was a member of the brotherhood. Between February 1936 and April 1937, newspapers and magazines such as the *Los Angeles Examiner*, the *San Francisco Chronicle*, *Newsweek*, *Time*, the *Christian Century*, and *Famous Detective Cases* took notice of the penitentes.[3] The majority of these periodicals ran feature stories and series that scandalized the brotherhood in an attempt to link penitente practices to the killing of Carl Taylor. This accusation was clearly articulated in a dramatic article that appeared in the *Cleveland News* shortly after the killing of Taylor. According to this newspaper account, it was quite clear that Carl Taylor's "clicking typewriter," revealing penitente "secrets," had been heard by members of the brotherhood, and consequently, Carl Taylor was now dead.[4]

The master narrative concerning the killing of Carl Taylor was driven by the desire to expose the deviant identity and practices of the penitente brotherhood to all of America. The penitente community was a "secret" and "strange mountain cult" enacted by "swart hot-eyed Mexicans and half breeds" that needed to be exposed. The hope was that the secretive "blood brothers" who reacted savagely toward meddling outsiders and who had been practicing their rite for hundreds of years were about to come to an end with their exposure from the Carl Taylor murder.[5] The two motives behind such a calculated exposé were to publicly display the evil wrath and vengeance of the brotherhood toward outsiders and to uncover the conflict over political power between the penitentes and the powers that be in the region.

One of the first stories to hit the press and scandalize the Taylor murder blamed the death directly on "penitente vengeance." The story depicted Taylor as an intellectual prophet who, despite the fact that his mouth had been "sealed" by cult vengeance, had completed his manuscript and was going to expose the "weird and bloody rituals of a strange religious sect":[6] "His discoveries of torture-rites in isolated mountain fastness did not die with him, it was learned today. Air mail letters stamped here Wednesday—a few hours before he was murdered—have been received by Taylor's friends in New York and unfold a harrowing account of the practices he investigated and of the dangers he realized he was incurring."[7]

These stories of vengeance were regularly corroborated by other brave souls who dared to expose the "bloody practices" of the penitentes. A musician by the name of Ira Leslie Allison was convinced that Taylor met the fate Allison had escaped eleven years earlier. The author of *Through the Years*, he recalled that members of the "cult" had personally vowed "vengeance" on him once his book was published: "I was threatened openly by bands of Penitentes. At length, I was warned that torture and death awaited me if I were captured; so mindful of the hideous spectacles I had witnessed in gathered materials for my book, I fled the region."[8]

Allison and others were cited in these stories to promote eyewitness accounts of the "blood-curdling ceremonial rituals of self torture" and transform them into believable and real events. Documenting firsthand eyewitness accounts was necessary to validate sensational penitente stories by vagabond writers, and scholars, for the reading public at large. In fact, during the 1950s, two curators from the Taylor Museum in Colorado Springs went as far as to develop a system for classifying eyewitness penitente accounts.[9]

Another important and constant theme surrounding the "cruel brotherhood" that arose with the Taylor murder was their unlimited "power" within the community. An article from this period entitled "Desert Golgotha: Penitentes Reenact Christ's Passion with Actual Crucifixion" informs us that if the willing penitente is subjected to a variety of tortures and dies, he will be buried secretly. However, if he lives, he is transformed into a hero and automatically bestowed with political power![10]

In a series of articles by the United Press that appeared in the *San Francisco Chronicle,* the penitente brotherhood was described as "exercising statewide power" through their political activities in the sovereign state of New Mexico.[11] In the first article of the series, entitled "Queer Religious Cult, Strange Rites in New Mexico: Slaying Linked to Penitentes," it was said that the death of Taylor "may officially bring to light the secret ritual and rigid code of brotherhood which has through its political power, avoided such publicity in the long years of existence in the United States."[12] According to the article, "Penitentes hailed into court for violation of the State laws, have been known to escape conviction despite overwhelming proof of guilt because of the presence of brothers on the jury."[13]

The logic presented here was that the penitentes were untouchable and could not be exposed due to their fierce political power: thank goodness for the media and the killing of Taylor, for now the brotherhood could be uncovered once and for all! Therefore, from the perspective of the media, it was critical that Modesto Trujillo's confession of having killed Carl Taylor solely for money not be accepted, for if believed, then the "queer practices" of the "penitente cult" would continue to live on. Furthermore, with acceptance of Trujillo's statement, "the season of sighs and suffering [will have] been renewed," and "cruel lashes" would continue to cut the "quivering backs of devotees." If Trujillo were believed, then "New Mexico, and the year 1936, will be robbed of a trial comparable only to another arraignment for witchcraft in Salem."[14]

A series of articles published by the *Los Angeles Examiner* presented a story by the self-proclaimed vagabond cameraman, Ronald Price. In this story, Price expressed his concern over the "grim control and power" penitentes had acquired over the years in the New Mexican region directly through penance and "unspeakable tortures." Price depicted the New Mexican region as "infested" with *moradas* that were ruled by the *hermano mayor* and said that the penalty for exposing "penitente secrets" was death by being buried alive![15]

Price was an important figure in the Taylor murder story because his photographic work served as the basis of a seventy-minute film that focused on the murder entitled *Lash of the Penitentes*. Also known as *The Penitente Murder Case*, this 1936 film opened with a dramatic on-screen script that directly linked the penitentes to the Taylor murder and said that as a result of the case, penitentes would now be exposed:

> The motion picture which you are about to see is brought to you not as a Hollywood production, but as the true representation of the tradition and customs performed for hundreds of years by this cult in pursuit of their beliefs. The processions, crucifixions, and flagellations were photographed at the risk of the cameramen's lives through long range lenses hidden in the mountains of the Penitente country. For years, the practices of the cult had

been carried-on unknown to the civilized world. It was not until 1936 that the murder of Carl Taylor, prominent writer, attracted public attention to the Penitentes rites. Carl Taylor, as the result of careful investigation, was prepared to bring to light the events depicted here. . . . The truth and authenticity of the scenes of the Penitente cult have been verified by leading newspapers and have appeared periodically in the press.[16]

In an attempt to reproduce the story of the Taylor murder, *Lash of the Penitentes* is about a journalist by the name of George Mack who arrives in the remote mountains of New Mexico to do a feature story on the penitentes. Mack has received a hot tip that the government is going to start investigating the penitente community, and he wants to get there "before they clean them out."

The film depicts northern New Mexico in the 1930s as lonely and silent. The mountains are said to have a weird unearthly beauty that reflects the changing moods of every hour. Penitente communities are characterized as peaceful until they feel a stranger has come among them to uncover their secrets and expose their rites to the glaring lights of publicity.

Mack hires a houseboy by the name of Chico Rubio, who is a penitente. Mack bribes the young man to show him the Good Friday ritual in which the chosen Cristo of the village is scourged and lashed to a cross. Soon afterward Chico is called before the penitente council. The council informs him that his actions have been discovered and that to atone for guiding the journalist, he must kill the meddler. While Mack sits at his desk finishing his story, Chico comes up behind and shoots him in the back. As Mack's body dramatically slumps over his completed manuscript, we observe the title page, which reads, "The Bloody Trail, by George Mack," as two large drops of blood stain the paper. Chico is arrested and confesses to the killing.

A film that can be dismissed as an "exploitation documentary" about the "fabled cult of New Mexico," *Lash of the Penitentes* ends with a disturbing racist scene. A large cross is seen burning in the dark of night, and

Movie poster for *The Lash of the Penitentes* (1936). Courtesy
Video Yesteryear.

the film's narrator states authoritatively, "Wake up America! Here in our
own country, we can see the very heart of Africa pounding against the ribs
of the Rockies!"

The film establishes some very important linkages between the Taylor murder and the press. For example, at the beginning, we are reminded that "leading publications" such as *Time, Liberty, American Detective,* and others have confirmed in their printed articles the scenes witnessed by Taylor. Toward the end of the film, a scene depicting a newsroom that is about to go to press fades into the sights and sounds of the running presses, and an on-screen script informs us that "the giant Press grinds on, feeding and thriving upon the adventure that lives in the hearts of men."

It is important to note that both the media coverage and the so-called documentary was met with protest by politicians and the print media within the state of New Mexico. In fact, Santa Fe's local newspaper called national newspaper coverage of the Taylor murder "Yellow Journalism" as it focused on the "spectacular" and "blood curdling" aspects of syndicated stories.[17] In addition, New Mexico governor Clyde Tingley wrote a letter of protest to the chairman of the National Board of Censorship in which he described *Lash of the Penitentes* as "cheap sensationalism" and vowed to ban the picture in New Mexico.[18]

Not all media coverage of the Taylor murder was overtly insensitive toward the penitente brotherhood. In an article entitled "Crucifixion by Request," Marcus Bach described members of the brotherhood as "deeply sincere" in their religious beliefs and practices. According to Bach, this sincerity could be confirmed by living among the people of northern New Mexico, as they attended to their sheep, weaved their blankets, or molded their pottery. At this level, outsiders could come to understand "what a redemptive part the torture and crucifixion plays in their daily lives."[19] Unfortunately, this insight was offered with the warning that if outsiders found themselves living among the people of northern New Mexico they might have to "fend for their life."

Another slightly sensitive portrayal from this period was offered by Mabel De La Mater Scacheri in her article, "The Penitentes: Murderous or Misguided?" With camera in hand while visiting various northern New Mexican communities, Scacheri was not entirely convinced that penitentes were "barbarous, savage" people. True, they were "primitive," but she could hardly look upon them as "dangerous wild beasts." In fact, Scacheri and her husband had experienced acts of kindness from the brotherhood in the form of food and lodging. From her perspective, the brotherhood was made up of rare, "perfectly sincere people who really act according to their deep beliefs."[20] The way to deal with these religious and often fanatical people, she wrote, was the "persuasive education of the children and young people among them," rather than by forcing the adults of this community toward any type of change.[21]

Having explored the master narrative that defined and shaped penitente identity and practices for mainstream American in the twentieth century, it is essential that we explore the roots of this explanatory framework. What was at the foundation of these stories? Why were all these stories based on flawed assumptions? In order to answer these questions it is necessary to go back to the earliest documented narratives of penitente life offered in a secular context, the stories of Josiah Gregg and Charles Lummis.

Josiah Gregg grew up along the Missouri frontier near Copper Fort at the turn of the nineteenth century. Described as a self-educated man with an "analytical" and "logical" mind, this "border boy" mastered the skill of observation by incessantly recording "everything he deemed worthy of remembrance" in his pocket notebooks.[22] At the age of twenty-five, under the orders of his doctor, Gregg found himself on his back on a wagon bed bound for Santa Fe, New Mexico, with a very serious case of consumption. This journey into the "pure air of the plains" would not only help cure his life-threatening illness, but more importantly, would transform him, by the age of thirty-eight, into a celebrated observer of and author on the customs and cultures of the prairies and of Mexican society.[23]

It soon became apparent that this adventure into a new world of "freedom from all the frustrations and irritations of past life" agreed with Gregg.[24] He was deeply attracted to the "wild unsettled and independent life of the Prairie trader," which made "perfect freedom from every kind of social dependence an absolute necessity of his being."[25] Seven days into the journey, he would remarkably recover his strength to the point that he was able to saddle his horse and ride a part of each day on the trail. Soon, Gregg was even strong enough to carry his share of the trailman's duties.[26] Gregg eventually became a successful proprietor in the Santa Fe trade. He made a total of eight trips across the prairies between 1831 and 1840, spending weeks or months at a time in Santa Fe.

It was in this new world of business along the Santa Fe Trail that his sense of commerce and his observational skills would merge. For Gregg, all of his trading trips were also scientific expeditions.[27] The analytical mind of his childhood transformed him into a shrewd businessman in this uncharted world among the Mexicans, but he also became a keen observer and recorder of the cultural lore of this unknown society. He was considered a scientist, writer, and "encyclopedist" of this newly discovered world. "There was much to study; there were many rewards for sober curiosity."[28]

As a successful merchant interested in the commerce of northern Mexico, he realized he had opportunities to observe the early history and condition of the people of New Mexico and give a full account of the origin and progressive development of the Santa Fe trade. He capitalized on this knowledge with the publication in 1844 of *Commerce of the Prairies,* considered the first systematic and comprehensive study on the history, resources, customs, and government of the prairie culture and of Mexican society. It was so popular that it went through five reprintings in ten years, and editions were published in England and Germany in 1845.

During one of his many visits to New Mexico, Gregg observed "acts of penance" during Holy Week in the town of Tomé and concluded that during this week, "sinners" could atone for their "sins" by partaking in these acts of penance: "It has been customary for great malefactors to propitiate Divine forgiveness by a cruel sort of *penitencia,* which generally takes place during the *Semana Santa.*"[29]

While in Tomé, Gregg's attention was arrested by a nearly naked man dragging a huge cross upon his shoulders, which he estimated to weigh over a hundred pounds. An immense stone swung from the middle of the cross, appended there to make the task more laborious.[30] Gregg was disgusted by the steady flow of blood from the back of the man bringing up the rear of the procession, who was being "lustily" whipped by another individual following close behind.[31] According to Gregg, the "penitents" he described were three of the most "notorious rascals in the country." In his estimation, they were granted "complete absolution" and "purification" of the past year's sins by annually submitting to this "species of penance," which allowed them to enter "afresh" into their old career of "wickedness and crime."[32]

As the first documented narrative of penitente life, Josiah Gregg's story is not the most recognized or enduring. The most famous vagabond narrative was constructed and developed by Charles F. Lummis toward the end of the nineteenth century, and some of the articles that focused on the Taylor murder drew from his scholarship.[33] Lummis became famous for his photographs of and accompanying story on the penitente community of San Mateo, New Mexico, published in the late nineteenth century.

Charles Lummis was born in Lynn, Massachusetts, on March 1, 1859, the son of Henry and Harriet (Fowler) Lummis. His father was a minister and teacher of languages who tutored the young Charles in Latin, Greek, and Hebrew. At the age of nineteen, Lummis entered Harvard University but was unsuccessful in completing his studies. On leaving college, he managed a 700-acre farm in Chillicothe and served as editor of a local newspaper between 1882 and 1884. In September 1884 he embarked on his famous "tramp across the continent" and arrived in Los Angeles, California, in February 1885.

During Holy Week of 1888, having suffered a stroke that paralyzed his entire left side while living in Los Angeles, Lummis moved to San Mateo, New Mexico, with the hope of regaining his health and moved in with his friend Manuel Cháves. There, in the lonely *cañones,* he first heard the "wild shriek" of the *pitero* (fife), which caused known men of "tried bravery" to flee from the sound in indescribable terror.[34] However, Lummis responded with the brave desire to photograph the series of events that he was about to witness: "I had been watching feverishly for Holy Week to come. No photographer had ever caught the Penitentes with his sun-lasso, and I was assured of death in various unattractive forms at the first hint of an attempt.[35] On Holy Thursday, Lummis hurried over to a hilltop to get near enough to the procession that had just begun but was confronted by an "openly hostile mob." His friend Don Ireneo Cháves and his two associates were successful in holding back the mob at gunpoint while Lummis photographed the "strange scene below."[36]

Having shrewdly wangled the *hermano mayor* with cigars and pictures, Charles Lummis was about to make history as the first photographer to capture a mock "penitente crucifixion" on Good Friday. The *hermano mayor* marked a spot thirty feet from the foot of the cross, where Lummis set up his tripod to photograph this historic event: "And there we stood facing each other, the crucified and I—the one playing with the most wonderful toy of modern progress, the other racked by the most barbarous device of twenty centuries ago."[37]

In an article about Lummis, David Roberts remarked that his "achievement" was impressive because he had use of only one arm when he took the photographs. Lummis's "nerve, energy, and persistence to capture images of places and customs that few people have ever seen" transformed him into a passionate champion of the Southwest and its people, wrote Roberts, who bestowed on him the title of Mr. Southwest.[38] Charles Lummis would eventually become an icon of American rugged individualism. He had trekked some 3,507 miles across America on foot with camera, pen, and pickax to encounter the first people of New Mexico. He was considered an "American polymath," who told stories of fighting wildcats and hammer-wielding prisoners.[39] By the end of his life, Charles Lummis had become an "Apostle of the Southwest," one of the first to "discover" this region of the United States.[40]

The vagabond narrative of New Mexico and the penitentes originated with the stories of Josiah Gregg and Charles Lummis. Both were represented as men who, due to physical ailments, were driven to discover their fame and fortune in new and exotic foreign lands. These are thrilling stories of danger and adventure in which the storyteller enters a new place and encounters unfamiliar people with strange religious practices. Their stories are the roots of a storytelling genre originating in the American Southwest in the late nineteenth century in which exotic cultures and their practices are the main focus. These stories took on the pragmatic function of informing the larger, dominant culture of these newly discovered people. In the story, the storyteller takes great personal risks in documenting his experiences with these unknown entities for the sake of informing Americans about the cultural oddities that persisted in their midst and possibly threatened the fabric of our civilization.

In these stories, penitente lore, stained by blood, crucifixions, and even murder, was part of a larger explanatory framework used by outsiders for inventing the American Southwest and transforming it into a "region of the imagination."[41] That framework helped establish a confused "hierarchy of value"[42] in which outsiders were attracted to the traditions and practices of southwestern cultures, but yet classified them as inferior when placed against the technological advances of the United States. This is particularly the case with Charles Lummis, whose penitente encounter occurred forty years after Gregg's and eight years after the arrival of the Atchison, Topeka, and Santa Fe Railroad in New Mexico.[43]

Technological advances in transportation, not to mention photography, would in Lummis's estimation bring an end to "unreclaimed" Hispano villages in New Mexico and to penitente traditions. He saw the railroad as the "death-knell" of the penitente order. The railroad made travel easier, bringing strangers to witness penitente rites and making it harder for penitentes to conceal their identity from church authorities. In his mind, the penitente brotherhood was not dead yet, but it was definitely on "its last leg."[44]

At the same time, Lummis and others were attracted to the simplicity and primitiveness of southwestern cultures. According to some scholars, this represented an antimodernist response to intense industrial development, massive European immigration, and rapid urbanization occurring in the eastern United States during this period.[45] Unfortunately, these sentiments were influential in understanding and explaining the cultures and traditions of the Southwest as primitive, stagnant, and isolated. In turn, the personal agency of these cultures was ignored, and their personal stories were silenced by the dominant culture.

It is important to underscore the fact that Charles Lummis is recognized as a pioneer in recording and portraying New Mexican Hispano culture with a great deal of empathy and sensitivity. Yet, it is also known that Lummis held strong reservations about members of the penitente community, labeling them "scattered knots of fanatics."[46] What is critical to remember is that Lummis's work would establish the framework for the hundreds of popular and scholarly publications that, like his own work, ignored the importance of penitente understanding and thinking about the sacred in their lives. And in the end, the collective consciousness of the dominant American culture would come to understand the brotherhood as a sacrilegious community that existed solely to possess vengeance and political power. This consciousness established the historical context for the Carl Taylor murder exposé.

With this perspective in mind, we are left with a most interesting dilemma concerning the power of story. Having heard the story of a devout penitente community that, guided by their beliefs, choose to sacralize the good example through acts of charity and prayer, and a counterstory that presents the penitentes as a profane and irreligious community, then the single most important question becomes, who do we believe? Which version of the story is the most accurate, and why? And finally, which story possesses the most currency in molding the penitente image of the Southwest?

3 Storytelling, Sacredness, Truth, and Power

I value fiction as much as academic writing, and I believe
that neither has a greater claim to the truth or responsi-
bility for telling the truth. I nonetheless believe that academic writers are distinguished from writers of fiction by
their agreement to ground their writing, their stories, in
certain kinds of evidence and to proceed toward the con-
clusions in terms of the conventions of academe. When I
found this evidence wanting, and the conventions skewed,
the distinction between writing and fiction was greatly
blurred, and I believe that in some respects this has raised
the questions most problematic to me.

—Sam Gill, *Mother Earth: An American Story*

The purpose of this chapter is to reveal the power of
the story: how *truth* (or for our purpose, *sacredness*)
about the penitentes in American history has been
constructed, validated, and maintained through relations of power and
with the force of vagabond and institutional master narratives. I seek to explain the impact of these master narratives and relations of power on both
the penitente story and the *lyrics* of penitente and Hispano spirituality.

How does American history serve as a guidepost for differentiating the
familiar from the unusual, or the sacred from the profane, for the region
and people of the Southwest? How does history mold and structure the

penitente story and endow it with meaning? How is the penitente brotherhood explained and interpreted in stories that are told about it, especially in light of the fact that conflicting images of the brotherhood have resulted from them? Answers to these questions lie in a review of the master historical narratives of the past, which framed and molded the penitente image in the Southwest prior to the Taylor murder story and the vagabond narratives of Josiah Gregg and Charles Lummis—namely, the institutional narratives constructed by the leaders of the Roman Catholic Church in nineteenth-century New Mexico, especially after 1850.

Penitentes and the Roman Catholic Church

Over the centuries, the New Mexican Hispano community has taught, and lived by, the values of mutuality, reciprocity, and self-determination, historically rooted in the sacred teachings of the penitente brotherhood. These sacred expressions are acts of charity achieved through prayer and the good example, reflective of a resilient people with a localized and practical faith that is both communal and devout. These penitente teachings and beliefs emerge from a historical context in which, under both the Spanish and Mexican Catholic church, the imprint of institutional Roman Catholicism and official Catholic sacraments were absent from the daily experiences and expressions of the people of New Mexico. What we have in its place is a practical religion based on personal access to God.[1] As a result, Hispano Catholicism evolves and develops as a ubiquitous religious tradition that is impossible to contain within the institutional boundaries of Roman Catholicism. Conversely, as Roman Catholic officials took interest in New Mexico, especially during the church's formative years in the nineteenth century, the hierarchy struggled to tell the story of Hispano popular religiosity, redefining and restructuring Hispano sacred expressions within the confines of official and institutional Catholicism. At the core of their official reformulations were representations of the penitente brotherhood.

The Penitente Story as Told by Bishop Zubiría

Don José Laureano Antonio Zubiría y Escalante was named bishop of Durango in 1831 and consequently made his first of three trips to examine the Church of New Mexico in 1833. Nominally, the region had been under the supervision of the diocese since 1729, but little had changed.[2] The area remained isolated, with little support or direction from clergy. There were fifteen priests in the region, eleven secular clergy *(curas),* and four aged and ill Franciscans *(frailes).*[3] According to Bishop Zubiría, the clergy neglected to care for the people and churches of New Mexico. In response, he mandated that the clergy be an example to their flock by living spiritual and moral lives.[4]

It was within this context that Zubiría responded to the presence of flagellants in the region. On July 21, 1833, in Santa Cruz de la Cañada, near present-day Española, New Mexico, Bishop Zubiría read a pastoral letter to his attentive flock calling for more native clergy who someday could instruct the laity thoroughly in the doctrines of the Holy Church. The bishop himself did not have enough priests to spare, and the Franciscan province in the Mexican capital was short of personnel. But in his mind, it was clear that without such instruction and guidance, the laity would fall into many errors.[5]

This lengthy pastoral letter, which he ordered to be read in all the parishes, condemned the presence

> of a brotherhood of Penitentes already existing for a goodly number of years, but without the authorization or even the knowledge of the Bishops, who certainly would never have given their consent for such a Brotherhood . . . since the excesses of most indiscreet corporal penances which they are accustomed to practice on some days of the year, and even publicly, are so contrary to the Spirit of Religion and the decrees of Holy Church. . . . We strictly command, and lay it strictly upon the conscience of our present and future pastors of this Villa, that they must never in future permit such reunions of Penitentes under any pretext whatsoever.[6]

In addition, the bishop ordered each and every penitente never again to consider himself a member of such a "Brotherhood of Penitence which we annul[led] and which must remain forever abolished."[7]

Before returning to Durango in October 1833, Zubiría reaffirmed with his clergy his directive to forbid these brotherhoods of penitence or "butchery." He envisioned a clergy in the territory of his administration that worked to prevent one of these brotherhoods from remaining in existence. As a form of compromise, the bishop was tolerant of "moderate penance" as long as it was not performed under the assemblage of a brotherhood that after his decree no longer had legal authorization. One who might "be moved by the spirit" to implement "the devices of penance that he may choose for mortification, and not for destruction" was permitted to do so as long as he kept his penance private.[8]

Zubiría returned to New Mexico in 1845 and asked that his pastoral letter be read once again in all churches. His third and final visit occurred in 1850, and to his dismay, he discovered that very little had changed. Unbeknownst to the bishop, the Diocese of Durango no longer exercised control over New Mexico, and major changes were in store for the future of the region and of institutional Catholicism.

The Penitente Story as Told by Bishop Lamy

With the signing of the Treaty of Guadalupe Hidalgo and the creation of the American Southwest, the Holy See of the Roman Catholic Church reacted favorably to a request from the Seventh Council of Baltimore and established the New Mexican territory as a vicariate, including present-day Arizona and southern Colorado, on July 19, 1850. Jean Baptiste Lamy, a recently ordained priest from France, was sent from the Ohio Valley as the first vicar apostolic in *partibus infidelium* (the region of the infidels). He was consecrated bishop and arrived in Santa Fe in 1851.

As the first leader of the newly established American Catholic Church in New Mexico, Bishop Lamy worked incessantly to establish and build a diocese in this recently acquired territory. Lamy built the institution of Catholicism by recruiting French clergy and building schools, hospitals, orphanages, churches, and cathedrals. In his mind, anything that threatened his organizational and doctrinal vision of his emerging Roman Catholic diocese needed to be challenged. In particular, any type of sacred expression that could not be contained within these institutional structures was to be controlled, redefined, and institutionalized.

Whereas Bishop Zubiría interpreted New Mexico Catholicism as lacking in official spiritual instruction and institutional leadership, Bishop Lamy saw the region as one that needed to be organized and structured as dictated by the newly acquired resident bishop of the American Catholic Church. As the first resident bishop and the local leader and interpreter of institutional American Catholicism, Lamy understood that it would take a long time to solve the problems of Catholicism in New Mexico. Ironically, he was a foreign bishop with a foreign clergy who was setting the agenda for religious expressions that were inherently a part of the history of the American Southwest and the Americas. At the center of his problems stood the penitente brotherhood and native New Mexican clergy.

The first set of rules for the penitentes, instituted by Bishop Lamy on October 27, 1856, were entitled "Rules that Must Be Observed by the Brothers of the Catholic Confraternity of Penitentes."[9] At the core of these twelve regulations was an order to "obey and respect" the Most Reverend Catholic Bishop Juan Lamy and his successors in all that they ordained. According to the bishop, the appropriate response by penitentes to such actions on his part was to perform acts of charity and obedience. Without obedience to the Supreme Pastor, that is, Lamy, one could be expelled from the brotherhood and deemed an unworthy member of the Catholic Church.[10] In addition, the *hermano mayor* was required to provide a membership list of the brotherhood to the local parish priest to monitor the conduct of membership.[11] These rules were to be signed by the parish priest and kept by the *hermano mayor*. Lamy

The cover of *The Old Faith and Old Glory*. Published by the Archdiocese of
Santa Fe, May 29, 1946. Used with permission of the Archdiocese of Santa Fe.

concluded by saying that he had minutely examined the prayers of the
brotherhood and found nothing contrary to the Catholic religion.[12]

The most significant statement against the penitentes by Jean Lamy
was presented in the form of a Lenten pastoral letter, written in 1879, four
years after Santa Fe became an archdiocese and Lamy was elevated to
archbishop. In this letter, published in a Spanish-language religious
weekly, *La Revista Católica*, Archbishop Lamy reprimanded the brother-

hood, who were alleged to have disobeyed the rules established by the Catholic hierarchy for partaking in "penitential practice" without first consulting their parish priests. According to the archbishop, members of the brotherhood continued to flagellate themselves to such a severe degree that many had become ill, and some had actually died. He reminded them that God was offended because the confraternity was not following the teachings of the church and should pay heed to the "maxim from the Holy Spirit" that "obedience is worth more than the sacrifices."[13] The archbishop concluded with a directive that "obedience to the authorities of the church and all that it dictates and prohibits on behalf of God" was paramount and "worth more than any form of penance practiced by some of the brotherhood." Such penance was deemed "blasphemous and unexemplary Roman Catholic behavior."[14]

It is significant that *Revista Católica* was published in Las Vegas, New Mexico, by Jesuit missionaries familiar with the brotherhood in the vicinity. As Marta Weigle underscores, this religious weekly served as a platform for Lamy's pastoral Letter, but more importantly, the archbishop's words of condemnation echoed sentiments published two years earlier by Jesuit missionaries. Furthermore, the publication helped popularize the idea that the penitentes were nineteenth-century remnants of the Third Order of St. Francis. This idea would have a direct and enduring impact on the way the American Catholic Church understood and dealt with the penitente brotherhood.[15]

St. Francis of Assisi lived between 1181 and 1226 and founded three orders. His initial group of followers, the First Order of St. Francis *(friars minor),* consisted of ordained priests and unordained brothers. The Second Order of St. Francis was comprised of women who formed communities of poor women known as Poor Clares as an alternative to traditionally large nunneries. The Third Order of St. Francis was made up of women and men "living in the world" who wished to live St. Francis's apostalate of peace.[16]

According to Fray Angélico Chávez, Archbishop Lamy and his successor, Archbishop Jean Baptiste Salpointe, incorrectly assumed that the penitente brotherhood had degenerated from the Third Order of St. Francis.[17] The penitentes were interpreted as a traditional Catholic confraternity that had gone astray. With the goal of weaning the brotherhood away from their practices, the hierarchy sought to bring them back in line with the rules and regulations of the institutional church. Therefore, the set of rules composed by Lamy and Salpointe were aimed at toning down practices of penance and convincing the brotherhood to consign their entire practice to strict privacy, and, instead, to stress good Catholic living by receiving the sacraments.[18] What is most important to emphasize here is that regardless of Third Order origins, the Hermanos Penitentes, as a popular expression, were still a threat to the legitimacy and longevity of institutional American Catholicism in the new American Southwest. Therefore, it follows that the hierarchy would do all in its power to strategically silence or redefine any expressions to the contrary.

In 1852 Lamy attended the First Plenary Council of the American hierarchy in Baltimore, referred to as the Baltimore Councils. The main purpose of the gatherings was to "reassert and justify the bishop's episcopal authority as being divinely charged by Christ."[19] It was concluded that the bishop's authority was all inclusive, with few if any boundaries. The bishop had ultimate authority over all property, real or personal, intended for the purpose of "divine services." American bishops were to claim docile obedience from the faithful when teaching the "truths of the faith" and when "prescribing rules of conduct."[20] With this type of orientation, a major objective for Archbishop Lamy was to bring not only the laity into compliance with these distinctively American ecclesiastical norms, but also the clergy.[21]

As a result of the plenary, Archbishop Lamy issued his own pastoral letter, asking priests to voluntarily contribute three-fourths of their parish revenue to the "common good" of the diocese. Revenues from the bishop's central fund were to be used at his discretion for church renovations and building schools.[22] The archbishop's ideal vision for his diocese was to instill in his clergy a communal espirit so that they would willingly and voluntarily tithe to this common cause.[23]

Not surprisingly, the obligation and collection of all tithes became a central source of tension in the diocese between the bishop and the native New Mexican clergy. The most famous of these conflicts was with Padre Antonio José Martínez, a major historic figure in New Mexican history. Padre Martínez played the role of scholastic father to native clergy and strongly influenced the citizenry of Taos. His life encompassed three distinct epochs of Mexican history. Don Antonio José Martínez was born on January 17, 1793, in Abiquiu, when New Mexican territories were under the control of the Spanish Crown. In 1822, one year after Mexican Independence, he was ordained a priest. The ideals of liberation offered by Mexico's first revolutionary hero, Padre José Miguel Hidalgo, deeply influenced the life of Padre Martínez and his views toward civil and ecclesiastical authority. In 1826 Martínez was assigned the pastorship in Taos, New Mexico, and soon after began schools for children at the Indian pueblos and the nearly Hispano villages. Eight years into his ministry, he established a preparatory seminary, from which twenty-two native priests were ordained. In 1846, Padre Martínez, now fifty-three, experienced the occupation of New Mexico by the United States.[24]

Early in 1853 Bishop Lamy wrote his first pastoral letter to the laity, outlining rules for reinstituting tithing. Tithing had been banned by Mexicans in 1833 with the Law of San Felipe. Individuals not in compliance with the bishop's new rules were denied the sacraments and deemed "outside the fold."[25] In the mind of Padre Martínez, this tithing mandate was a hardship for his flock because of the burden it placed upon the poor. Interestingly enough, as a young priest, Martínez was at the forefront of the movement to abolish church tithing, which culminated in the Law of San Felipe.[26]

In a second pastoral letter, issued approximately one year later, Bishop Lamy evoked the "fifth precept of the church" to support his claim that all families must "support the church materially."[27] In July 1856 it was reported that in response to Lamy's letter, Padre Martínez and his friend Padre Lucero of Arroyo Hondo were working on an article for the local newspaper calling for the abolition of tithes. When the article appeared, in September, Padre Lucero was suspended by the bishop because of his close association with Martínez.[28]

On October 23, 1856, a Basque priest by the name of Dámso Taladrid informed Bishop Lamy that Martínez was celebrating Mass in his private oratory. Taladrid had been assigned to Taos earlier in the year to replace Martínez, who had written to Lamy that he wanted to retire. Lamy suspended Padre Martínez the very next day, depriving him of canonical faculties and saying that the suspension would be in affect until he retracted his newspaper article. Martínez protested the bishop's actions and in a letter written in November 1856 argued that his publication on the matter of tithing was protected by guarantees of "republican free speech."[29] Five additional pleas were ignored by Bishop Lamy, and in June 1857 formal excommunication procedures against Padre Martínez were set in motion. Within five months, Padre Antonio José Martínez was formally excommunicated by the Santa Fe diocese.[30]

At the core of Archbishop's Lamy's vision for the Archdiocese of New Mexico was his intention to bring the native penitente brotherhood and clergy in line with the teachings of the Roman Catholic hierarchy. For Archbishop Lamy, it was all about obedience to his episcopal authority. This is evident in a succinct church history of New Mexico written at the end of the nineteenth century. A priest, writing for the Congregation de Propaganda Fide, wrote that Archbishop Lamy's most significant contribution to the archdiocese and its people was Roman Catholic "instruction and the frequent reception of the Sacraments." As a result, "immorality [had] been removed from the family," and instead, "morality, virtue, and religion had been made to flourish in the desert of past passions."[31]

For some scholars, the historical record does not indicate that Bishop Lamy worked to eliminate the penitente brotherhood. Rather, as stated above, his main concern was maintaining authority in all organizational and doctrinal matters pertaining to the church. Projecting a good image of the church for civil authorities and non-Catholics is what led Lamy to establish penitente rules.[32] Others believe that the bishop did all in his power to eliminate the movement. Frances Leon Swadesh claims that Lamy instituted the "practice of verification" before administering the sacraments in order to prevent penitentes from receiving communion unless they first renounced their membership in the brotherhood.[33] What is clear is that Hispano Catholic expression rooted in communal and experiential tradition ran contrary to the institutional Catholic vision of Bishop Lamy.

One of Jean Baptiste Lamy's final acts as archbishop of New Mexico, in 1885, was to write his last lenten pastoral letter, directed at Pope Leo XIII's recognition and ecclesiastical support of lay Catholic associations. This papal acknowledgment, an attempt by the church to embrace such associations, was a direct response to a predominantly American Catholic labor union known as the Knights of Labor, which, according to some church leaders, was a secret society. In his pastoral letter, Archbishop Lamy chose to ignore the inferred support of the Catholic hierarchy for lay societies and instead emphasized their negative elements, such as secrecy. Such a perspective would be embraced by Archbishop Lamy's successor and have long-term consequences for the penitente brotherhood in their official relationship with the institutional church.[34]

The Penitente Story as Told by Bishop Salpointe

In 1885 Jean Baptiste Salpointe was appointed coadjutor to the archbishop of Santa Fe and upon the resignation of Archbishop Lamy the same year was appointed the second archbishop of Santa Fe. Originally from France, Archbishop Salpointe spent the majority of his pastoral life in the American Southwest, first as a priest in Mora, New Mexico, and later as vicar apostolic in Arizona. One of his first acts as archbishop was to establish rules for the Society of the Brotherhood of Our Father Jesus in which he warned against the "deleterious influence of secret . . . societies."[35] Like his predecessor, Salpointe's rules were in response to Pope Leo XIII's ecclesiastical vision of recognizing lay Catholic associations. Two years earlier, in May 1883, the pope had called for a revival of lay associations, including the Third Order of St. Francis.

In March 1886, Salpointe issued and distributed a circular with the pope's *Rules of the Society of the Third Order of St. Francis* to all priests, proclaiming that the penitentes had originated from the Third Order of St. Francis and would have to return to it in order to obtain all of the "indulgences" promised by the pontiff.[36] The problem with this proclamation and perspective was that the penitentes were seen as a traditional Catholic confraternity that had gone astray and needed to be brought back in line with the rules and regulations of the institutional church. Without rules and regulations, the brotherhood would neither survive nor prosper. Not surprisingly, the archbishop's circular emphasized "obedience" to "God's earthly vicar" over "sacrifice."[37] Of great significance is that public flagellation and cross-bearing, not mentioned by the pope, were included in Salpointe's circular.

At the first Synod of the Archdiocese of Santa Fe, led by Archbishop Salpointe in June 1888, the brotherhood was firmly condemned and described as "nothing else but a political society." The archbishop urged his pastors to guide this degenerate group into embracing the Rules of the Third Order or else deprive them of the sacraments and refuse to celebrate Mass in their chapels until they amended their ways.[38]

In his next circular, dated March 31, 1889, the archbishop continued to underscore the link between the brotherhood and the Third Order of St. Francis. He highlighted the fact that, as written in his circular of 1886, public flagellation in his diocese was strictly prohibited. He explained that those who continued to disobey must incur the same censures imposed upon other flagellant groups throughout history.[39]

Archbishop Salpointe issued his last circular on February 7, 1892, in response to a group of brothers from San Miguel County who petitioned the archbishop to be recognized as obedient subjects willing to embrace his rules. He characterized these men as dishonest and unsubmissive "sons of the Church," solely in search of political power, and accused them of having contrived their own personal set of penitente rules without his permission or blessing. The archbishop was clear and direct in this circular regarding his dealings with the penitente brotherhood, saying that all penitentes had to subject themselves to Archbishop Salpointe's authority as articulated in his circulars of 1886 and 1889. Furthermore, if they ignored the bishop's authority, they would be considered "rebels to their mother the Church, and that until such time that they submit," they would "be deprived of the reception of the Sacraments."[40] Jean Baptiste Salpointe resigned as archbishop of Santa Fe on January 7, 1894, less than two years after writing his final circular. Yet his rules and regulations would have a lasting impact on the brotherhood well into the twentieth century.

The argument has been made that tensions between the institutional church and the brotherhood were rooted in issues of authority and not based on cultural or racial differences. Parallels are drawn between Zubiría and Lamy to argue that both church leaders simply sought to reinforce the rules of the church.[41] While such a statement is accurate, we cannot diminish the impact of these rules. Zurbiría came to the New Mexico without the institutional and symbolic resources necessary to enforce his dictates, and right before a major war that radically changed the political, economic, and cultural landscape of New Mexico. In comparison, Lamy and his successors arrived in New Mexico when it was a newly established American territory, with a new set of rules and the full support of the American Catholic hierarchy. His vision, and that of his successors, would have a lasting impact on Roman Catholic expression in the Southwest.

Whereas both the institutional church and the penitente brotherhood are representations and expressions of Roman Catholicism in New Mexico during the nineteenth century, the review of the church's institutional narratives presented here confirms that the Roman Catholic Church never sought to establish a relationship with the Hermandad. Penitente sacred stories or lyrics were never recognized as a legitimate dimension of Roman Catholicism, nor even considered a cornerstone on which to build the institutional church of the American Southwest. The penitentes represented nothing more than a cultural aberration or remnant that was meaningless for an emerging Catholicism defined by authority and power. After the U.S. occupation, racial, ethnic, and cultural differences became markers of distinction not only for American Catholic officials, but also for Protestant missionaries seeking to introduce and reproduce American Protestant hegemony in the region.[42] Consequently, the penitente brotherhood was not granted official church recognition until 1947, under the leadership of Archbishop Edwin Vincent Byrne and Hermano Miguel Archibeque—over fifty years after Archbishop Salpointe's circular of 1892.[43] Unfortunately, the church's institutional narratives of the nineteenth century instead sought to silence or at least reform what in the eyes of the church was nothing more than an excessively flagellant and cross-bearing community with political aspirations. Interestingly enough, the penitente image presented in the vagabond narratives of nineteenth- and twentieth-century America would be disturbingly similar.

Institutional Catholicism, Vagabond Narratives, and Penitente Scholarship

The stories of Josiah Gregg and Charles Lummis were part of a vagabond genre that introduced penitente identities and practices to twentieth-century mainstream America through the Carl Taylor murder story. These stories of risk and danger were told by storytellers who traveled to strange lands to discover exotic cultures and practices and expose them to the civilized world.

Several scholars have explained the negative portrayals of the penitentes in the vagabond narratives as the creation of Protestant storytellers with biases against Roman Catholicism.[44] For example, in *Commerce of the Prairies,* Josiah Gregg defined New Mexican Catholicism as "superstitious blindness" in which "people believe that every one of their legion of canonized saints possesses the power of performing certain miracles."[45] Penitente scholars have also cited the infamous work of the Reverend Alexander Darley and his controversial attack on Roman Catholicism.[46]

However, closer examination of these vagabond narrative reveals that their stories were informed by the narratives of the institutional church. Consider how Charles Lummis, in *The Land of Poco Tiempo,* informs us that in the early days, the penitentes were too strong to be "excommunicated at one fell swoop." Eventually, the Catholic church went to work, "lopping off a head here and a head there in a quiet way, which carried its full lesson without provoking rebellion." He concludes by informing us that church "policy has been a successful one and has been unflinchingly maintained."[47] Clearly, the actions of the institutional church had a direct impact on the penitente image given in the vagabond narrative. By drawing attention to the penitente problem, the institutional church and its institutional narratives created an image of the brotherhood that would inform and influence bohemians, vagabond writers, and eventually scholars.

Furthermore, the distinction between Protestant and institutional Catholic interpretations of the brotherhood in the nineteenth century is difficult to establish when one considers that both of these groups consisted of non-Hispano outsiders who interpreted and judged native Hispano traditions through the same glasses. Randi Jones Walker wrote that Protestant missionaries and the Roman Catholic hierarchy possessed similar views of native New Mexican clergy. Along with his Protestant adversaries, Bishop Lamy saw native priests as immoral and dishonest, having led the New Mexican people to "licentiousness, sensual indulgence, worldliness, and idolatry."[48] Apparently, constructions of race and ethnicity were more pervasive than constructions of the sacred, especially if images of the sacred were rooted in race. For example, Reverend William Barton wrote early in the twentieth century, "I was told of one man who, before employing a [New] Mexican, would compel him to remove his shirt, and if he found his back scarred would refuse to employ him."[49] The logic was that any Mexican or Hispano from this region might be a flagellant.

Penitente Scholarship: Third Order Theory

The institutional narratives of Bishops Zubiría, Lamy, and Salpointe; the vagabond narratives of Josiah Gregg, Charles Lummis, and Carl Taylor; and the scholarship of Dorothy Woodward, Fray Angélico Chávez, Marta Weigle, William Wroth, and J. Manuel Espinosa have all addressed the origins of the penitente brotherhood. More importantly, the majority of these storytellers have sought to explain penitente origins by examining the historical connection between the brotherhood and the Third Order of St. Francis.

An important article by J. Manuel Espinosa reveals that the origins of the penitentes remains a point of contention because of the absence of official documentation. The Third Order theory is at the crux of the debate. Espinosa provides a useful review of the three competing theories.[50]

The most recent origin theory was advanced by William Wroth, who asserts that the penitente brotherhood began as an independent *cofradía* (confraternity) named the Hermanos de la Sangre de Cristo (Brotherhood of the Blood of Christ), established in Spain and introduced into New Mexico via Mexico sometime before the 1830s. According to Wroth, the Brotherhood of the Blood of Christ was established in both Spain and Mexico as early as the sixteenth century. Wroth's theory is based on recently discovered correspondence from Padre Martínez to Bishop Zubiría, dated February 21, 1833, in which Martínez denounced penitente public processions in Taos during the Lenten season. In his letter, Martínez referred to this group as the Hermandad de la Sangre de Cristo, as Zubiría did in his response. For Wroth, this is a clear indication that the name Brotherhood of the Blood of Christ was the original name of the penitentes and that the Hermandad was established independently from the Third Order.[51] Wroth disagrees with the Third Order theory mainly because he claims that the functions of the Franciscan Third Order were significantly different from those of the Mexican brotherhood. The Third Order sought to emulate the life of the friars, whereas penitential confraternities focused particularly on penance. He also addressed organizational and ritual differences.[52]

In 1954 Fray Angélico Chávez purported that the penitentes originated in sixteenth-century Spain as the Brotherhood of Nuestro Padre Jesús Nazareno and were introduced into New Mexico via Mexico in the late eighteenth century. According to Chávez, it is possible that the brotherhood has roots in Central America, but it is certain that no historical connection with the Franciscans or Third Order exists. Drawing from the reports of Fray Francisco Atanasio Domínguez in 1777 and Bishop Zubiría's decree of 1833, Chávez argues that the penitente brotherhood began sometime between 1790 and 1810. He claims that Domínguez, a learned Franciscan priest from Mexico City, was commissioned to make a detailed description of all the New Mexico missions, their buildings, religious programs, and religious societies. Yet nowhere in the report is there any mention of penitentes. In contrast, Bishop Zubiría's decree of 1833 condemns corporal penance and a brotherhood of penance. The bishop stated that these penitentes had been in existence for a "goodly number of years" ("ya bastante años atrás"). Chávez deduces that the brotherhood originated between 1790 and 1810, a half century prior to the American occupation, and that it was definitely not a movement inherited from the first two centuries of New Mexico's existence as a Spanish kingdom.[53] Instead, Chávez attributes the penitente movement to the "spirit of primitive Christian penance" inherent in the "Spanish soul."[54]

Finally, J. Manuel Espinosa, dissatisfied with both Wroth's and Chávez's theories, offers his own origin theory based on a revised version of the traditional theory, first advanced by Marta Weigle. He contends that the penitente brotherhood represents a continuation of the Franciscan Third Order in the second half of the eighteenth century. According to Espinosa, the penitentes evolved in northern New Mexico and southern Colorado from the Franciscan-sponsored Third Order of St. Francis. Citing the personal penitential practices of Fray Francisco de Jesús María Casañas, Espinosa argues that Father Casañas undoubtedly influenced the more devout New Mexicans in the late seventeenth century. Prior to his missionary work in New Mexico, Father Casañas carried out public penances during Holy Week in the Franciscan convent in Querétaro, Mexico. Among his numerous acts of penance, he made many walks barefoot, carrying a thick cross over his shoulders, with a coarse rope around his neck and a crown of thorns pressing against his temples.[55] Prior to being killed by "rebel Indians" at the mission in Jémez in 1696, it is recorded that Casañas prayed for his attackers to crucify him at a cross he had erected so he could die as Christ died.[56]

Espinosa claims that as the number of Franciscans in northern New Mexico steadily declined in the late eighteenth century, many of the faithful took the performance of some religious services into their own hands: "Without the guidance of Franciscan clergy, and without official authorization from the hierarchy in Mexico, the Penitentes had gradually emerged, building on the Third Order model, each group of brothers under the leadership of a locally elected hermano mayor, the traditional title of the leader of a Third Order chapter."[57] In sum, Espinosa provides us with two significant findings regarding the origin and purposes of the penitentes: the central purpose of the Hermandad was to partake in Holy Week exercises commemorating Christ's passion and death; and the penitentes, in their own way, perpetuated Lenten penitential practices that the members of the Third Order had learned from their Franciscan mentors in seventeenth-century New Mexico.[58]

Espinosa provides us with key historical evidence about the origins of the penitente brotherhood. Yet one cannot help noticing the direct impact of the institutional narratives of the church in shaping the penitente story as told by scholars. It is important to recall the fact that Bishop Salpointe, the first to clearly document and promote the Third Order theory in explaining the origins of the penitente brotherhood, was attempting to bring penitentes in line with the rules and regulations of the institutional church. From this perspective, the brothers were seen as unorthodox members of the Third Order and the Roman Catholic Church. The circulars he left behind are the institutional narratives that tell us this version of the penitente story. Furthermore, as Espinosa's work illustrates, the Third Order theory persists as one of the most important stories to be told about the brotherhood by contemporary scholars and researchers.

It is a story about a religious group that, although devout and obedient, was without official guidance and regulations, and deviated from the institutional norms of Roman Catholic expression. As a result, no effort is made by the storytellers to understand the penitente brotherhood on its own terms. Instead, it has been discussed and interpreted in the shadow of institutional Catholicism. In the late nineteenth century, Bishop Salpointe established and laid out the scholarly apparatus for understanding the most important aspects of the penitente sacred world. Not only did this perspective inform Third Order scholarly theory, it also influenced and sustained penitente stories of isolation and flagellation.

Isolation Theory

Researchers who claim that the penitentes deviated from the Third Order of St. Francis base their thesis on the isolated region and people of New Mexico. This isolation is usually cast in a negative light and is assumed to have had negative consequences for the New Mexican people and their human agency. The story tells of a community that has remained on the "fringe" of the New World,[59] "outside the American mainstream,"[60] and a "cultural island in a surrounding modern Anglo influenced sea."[61] In this interpretation, isolation preserved "Old World customs"[62] and postponed assimilation into the mainstream culture. Whereas it is true that the New Mexican experience was one of isolation and struggle, another story needs to be told, one that describes the self-determination of a people who, despite the odds, continue to persevere and maintain their traditions. Within the sacred realm, isolated New Mexican communities should be recognized as producing bold and creative ways of teaching and passing on religious faith through family and friends. These teachings ought to be recognized and celebrated as popular religious expression, and not as deviancy.

Penitentes as Flagellants

The image of the penitente as flagellant prevails as the central story being told by scholars and researchers.[63] This assumption is illuminated by J. Manuel Espinosa, who consistently classifies penitente identity and history as manifestations of corporeal penitential practices.[64] This representation is imagined through the historical remnants of institutional narratives that remain the official record on penitente experiences and expressions. Unfortunately, this historical record is incomplete and tells us only part of the story. The identification of the penitente in the historical accounts provided by Espinosa and others is drawn predominantly from descriptions of flagellant practices. Such an approach begs the question: is it possible that penitentes existed throughout New Mexican history who were not expressly flagellants? If such a scenario is possible, then we must ask ourselves, how were such individuals interpreted in an institutional narrative in which the main objective was to document flagellant behavior?

The scholarly story presented by Espinosa assumes that flagellation and penance are synonymous. Such a historical approach to the study of New Mexican penitentes is problematic. We must keep in mind that in his circular of 1892, the last, Salpointe claimed that a "good number of [penitentes] have correctly interpreted our intention . . . by subjecting themselves to what we had prescribed in our circular of 1886 and 1889."[65] What is known about the spiritual and religious character of these individuals, and how does the historical record bear it out? Another point to consider is that, according to Wroth, in sixteenth-century Spain, the Brothers of Blood practiced self-mortification, while the Brothers of Light only carried candles while marching.[66] According to Ramón Gutiérrez, these confraternities were distinguished along status and racial/ethnic lines in eighteenth-century New Mexico.[67] What else is known about the Brothers of Light, particularly as a spiritual and religious community? As it currently stands, the official story is incomplete. The flagellant penitente story objectifies the brotherhood and silences the story of sacred experiences and expressions in the everyday experiences of the Hermandad. In the final analysis, it ignores the deeper understanding of *penitencia* in the lives of the brotherhood.

Toward a New Penitente Story

Institutional, vagabond, and scholarly narratives directly impact the way in which truth and sacredness in the lives of the Hermanos Penitentes have been constructed, validated, and maintained throughout American history. The Third Order theory, first prescribed through the institutional narrative of the official church, influenced the penitente story told in the ensuing vagabond and scholarly narratives. It is a story that highlights the negative qualities of isolation, but more importantly, emphasizes flagellant images of the brotherhood that remain in stories of the contemporary period. The most recent literature published on the subject continues on the same track: "The high point in penitente worship is the re-creation of Christ's passion on the cross through a range of activities including self-mortification of the flesh and emulation of Christ's Crucifixion."[68]

The persistent representation of the Hermanos Penitentes as flagellants is understood by identifying those who have had power over and controlled access to the official story. As an official story, it is imbued with power because it remains the most often-told story and consequently has been placed prominently in the consciousness of an entire society. As a result, truth and sacredness are shaped by the formulations and interpretations put forth by tellers of the official story. The Third Order theory emerged as the most prominent theme in the institutional narrative after 1850 because the newly installed Catholic church moved to reform or silence movements such as the penitente brotherhood that ran counter to the institution. Such attempts attracted the imaginations of outsiders who, with an antimodernist response to intense social change in the East, sought to uncover strange and exotic cultures in unchartered territories. As the majority of scholars embarked on "studying" the brotherhood, their strategies for uncovering truth and knowledge about this community led them to the official institutional and vagabond stories that sustained the flagellant view and became a major focus in scholarship about the penitentes of New Mexico.

Consequently, the archaic patterns of spiritual creativity encoded in both the lyrics and stories by penitentes about their spirituality would go unrecognized or misunderstood by the dominant culture. Little is known about the ways in which penitentes experienced, reflected, and expressed their spirituality. Instead, the dominant perspective would restrict their understanding of penitente sacred expressions to Lenten rituals. For the most part, the relationship between the spiritual and material worlds as defined by the brotherhood in the daily life of New Mexican communities would be ignored.

The truth of the matter is that penitente sacred expressions are more profound than simple ritual. Penitente beliefs have provided a social imperative for New Mexican communities throughout history.[69] The social obligations and arrangements in these communities have historically been rooted in religion. Through charity, prayer, and the good example, sacred beliefs in the penitente tradition represent practical examples of human agency that have been sustained in stories told by the community.

4 The Story of Penitente Spirituality as Practical Christianity

Several years ago, a group of us wanted to build a *morada* on the outskirts of town with less than two months before the beginning of Lent. Any carpenter or engineer is going to tell you that to square a piece of land from nothing is going to bring about major hardships [*duras penas*]. It's not easy! I don't care how good you are, you understand? And life has taught me, having worked construction, how to square a foundation.

I design my corners, I place the batter board, more or less where I want them, and then I run string held by nails. I move and move the nails until I get a perfect square; but you spend your entire day doing this! And if you don't do it right, then the rest is not going to come out. It behooves you to spend the whole day doing this so it comes out perfect. And I mean perfect, because if you are off by just a bit, then the sheetrock will not fit!

One day, four older *hermanos* and I, all who have since passed away, took block out to this location for the footing of the building. We figured we would take the blocks to leave them there, since our main task for the day was to square the foundation. When we arrived, we decided where we wanted to build the *morada,* and we began to measure. So I put down the batter board to design the corners. We had precut them a foot bigger with an electric saw back home so we could run the string. I remember thinking to myself, here is where the hard part begins, you know, to square it. With nails, we set the string, and went off to have some coffee we had brought, to delay the headaches that faced us to square it.

Look! I am telling you the truth [*la mera verdad*], and this might be hard to believe: we didn't have to move the string anymore! It was perfect! In fact, I was shaking my measuring tape to see if something was wrong with it. We measured from one corner to the other and it was perfect. The *hermanos* and I looked at one another and measured it again and again you know. Well because of that, we began to dig the footings and we were able to put down the block that same day! As a result, we were able to use the *morada* by Ash Wednesday. I know this sounds unbelievable, but then again, this is how my Father God [Tata Dios] works! When you are doing the work of my Father God, it is crazy for you to believe that He will not help. Why shouldn't He, it's for Him! God will help you so your task won't be so difficult.[1]

Hermano Santiago Luna's story of the building of the *morada* is significant because it identifies and illustrates the prominence of practical Christianity within the penitente sacred world. Practical Christianity is a practical form or style of Christianity rooted in human agency. It connotes an efficacious style of communal spirituality in which the sacred worth of an individual is dictated by their effectiveness in simultaneously sustaining and enhancing the spiritual as well as material aspects of a community. The spiritual virtues of practical Christianity are measured by their useful and purposeful application within the material or empirical world. In this context, spirituality becomes real through human agency.

The underlying foundation and major assumption offered by this perspective is the belief that sacred experiences and expressions emerge directly through the actions of people. As emphasized throughout this study, my methodological focus is on the power of story and storytelling as a way of uncovering this unique form of sacred human agency. In sum, stories about the sacred provide us with the *lyrics* necessary for guiding the spiritual creativity of communities because they are grounded in the actions of a people.

Stories of practical Christianity uncover the "experiential scripts" of penitente religious expressions and reveal to us how the sacred is understood, constructed, and pursued by the penitente brotherhood.[2] The practical implications of these stories are experienced, interpreted, and understood in the social world where the power of the sacred, with all its implications, becomes meaningful through its ability to inform the purposive actions of a people. This *sacralization* of purposive human action attributed to the penitente sacred world must be understood within the larger historical and regional context of New Mexico.

As skilled carpenters and construction workers, Santiago Luna and the four older *hermanos* realized that it would take nothing short of a miracle for them to finish the *morada* before Lent, especially since they would have to set a structural foundation outside of town without the convenience of electricity. From this story we come to understand the ways in which a community calls upon the sacred for the perseverance and knowledge required for accomplishing designated tasks *(tareas)* faced by individuals within the material world. Furthermore, the sacred, which operates simultaneously in both the spiritual and material worlds, is distinguished by its *practical* application and utility. In short, the materiality of the social world influences the way people do religion, and the way religion should be done.

Of greatest significance however, is how this story illustrates the human agency of practical Christianity encapsulated in the sacred triad of penitente spirituality: charity, prayer, and the good example. In the penitente world, doing prayer or praying, *haciendo oración,* represents an overt charitable act or action on behalf of the brotherhood and the larger community. In this story, the act of building a *morada* in preparation for the Lenten season is itself an act of prayer. The *morada* is a sacred abode that has been at the root and core of Hispano culture and community for centuries. Therefore, the act of constructing this *morada* fulfills a larger symbolic objective of creating and preserving community for the people of the region through prayer as defined in the penitente's sacred world.

The penitente act of prayer is a charitable act, or *obra de caridad,* because it is through time, physical labor, and "sacrifice" expended on the creation of a *morada* that the brotherhood seeks to instill the values of mutuality and reciprocity for themselves and the community.[3] The performance of prayer through acts of charity culminates in the sacralization of the good example, or *buen ejemplo,* for all in the community to witness and emulate since they are considered actions with "good intentions." In addition, because Father God intervened in the creation and construction of this sacred site, the penitente community is able to testify to the power of the sacred in their personal lives as members of the brotherhood.

The dimensions of practical Christianity must be understood as the most efficient and effective ways by which New Mexican penitentes have shaped their spirituality in historically isolated communities without support from the institutional church. Characterized by its communal and popular sacred expressions, practical Christianity in the penitente's sacred world captures the ways in which a community has creatively learned to sustain itself both spiritually and materially, and in the process, to strengthen New Mexican communities.

Women have played an important and powerful role as conveyors and keepers of the faith in the history of Hispano New Mexico. Hispanas have been central to the socialization of believers and the dissemination of the faith as described by Hermano Santiago Luna in chapter 1. We recall that Doña Petra, Hermano Luna's teacher of religion, in a very real and practical way, passed on the traditions, faith, and stories of Hispano

Catholicism. In concert with the Hermandad, these women were links to the sacred through their teachings and human agency. Not surprisingly, the dimensions of practical Christianity identified in the penitente sacred world are also evident in the sacred experiences and expressions of these women's lives.

Writers and scholars have documented a range of stories regarding "penitente women," or *penitentas,* in New Mexico beginning in the nineteenth century. Based on the personal knowledge of J. B. Cisneros, of Taos, Marta Weigle tells us about the Women's Fraternal Society, which emerged around 1895 near Questa, New Mexico, comprised of the wives of male penitentes.[4] Another writer identifies a group of penitentas as "Beatas," active during the early twentieth century in Clovis, New Mexico. Jo Roybal Izay informs us that these Beatas would gather in the homes of the members for religious services. She offers no explanation of the meaning of the name.[5] Stories have also been gathered about women in leadership roles within the penitente male world, for example, Scholástica Chacón, a female auxiliary, or *auxiliadora,* who is said to have been named *hermano mayor* of a *morada* in San Rafael, Colorado; and Guadalupe Trujillo, from La Posta, Colorado, recognized by the Hermandad of this region as an honored person and *rezadora* (prayer leader) in the brotherhood.[6]

However, traditionally, the role of women in the penitente world has been predominantly that of female auxiliaries in the local *morada,* the wives and relatives of the *hermanos.* In Costilla, New Mexico, and San Luis, Colorado, the role of women within formal auxiliaries has been to prepare meals for the brothers, care for the sick, clean the interior of the *morada,* and assist in the burial of the dead.[7]

Certain writers refers to the women of these auxiliaries as Carmelitas, also known as Verónicas and Terceras (Tertiaries). They are described as women who combine piety with humanitarian acts and have "dedicated themselves to Jesus Christ."[8] In addition to the activities described above, these women focused their attentions on church-related activities such as

Funeral procession, Mora, New Mexico, ca. 1895. Photo by Tom Walton.
Courtesy Museum of New Mexico, Neg. No. 14757.

embroidering altar cloths with religious representations, making straw-inlaid crosses, and dressing the *santos*.[9] Dressed traditionally in dark clothing with a black head covering, Carmelitas partook in the dramatization of the meeting between Jesus and his mother on the way to Calvary, known as The Encounter (El Encuentro), which is reenacted during the Lenten season.

We have the story of María Dolores Córdova from Trujillo, New Mexico, described as a dedicated Carmelita and *partera* (midwife). She frequently cleaned the local church, dressed the *santos,* and sang *alabados* on feast days such as that dedicated to Our Lady of Carmel, every sixteenth of July. Also referred to as an *hermana,* she worked diligently to create and maintain a sense of community for all.[10]

Not surprisingly, the closer these "religious women" are linked to the penitente tradition, the more we find them associated with the flagellant male image. The majority of penitentas are identified and defined through their involvement in flagellant activity. For example, the women of Questa described above were said to "go up to the mountains or to any other secret place and whip themselves."[11] Marta Weigle introduces us to the notion of "inconspicuous penance" by penitentas, which, in her estimation, may or may not be indicative of official brotherhood status. This includes activities such as walking with rice in their shoes or wearing a penitential bracelet of cactus *(cilicio)* underneath their clothing. Such practices are defined as inconspicuous penance on the logic that penitential acts are part of a larger, more conspicuous Roman Catholic tradition.

Such a notion begs the question: if such a perspective is accurate, then why doesn't it also apply to their male counterparts? In other words, in the stories that have been told about them, why is corporal penance the single most important activity by which to define male penitentes and differentiate them from other religious groups in American history? The response is rather obvious. If this were not the case, then the entire flagellant image of New Mexican penitentes as created by the master narratives of the dominant culture would cease to exist. Accordingly, gender comparison of women and men in the penitente sacred world can lead to some important topics for future research in the understanding and interpretation of the penitente community.[12]

We discover that, just as in the stories that have been told about penitentes, our understanding and thinking about the sacred in the lives of penitentas has been ignored and consequently silenced. The majority of these stories lack a discussion about the sacred expressions and experiences of these female practitioners of the faith. Furthermore, because the sacred lived experiences and expressions of these women have never been thoroughly documented, their contributions to the Hispano sacred world remain unknown.

It is rare to hear stories like the one told by a *hermano* who refers to his mother as a penitenta filled with wisdom and recalls her singing verses about the *morada* "in a very profound way."[13] For this *hermano*, his mother was a "spiritual guide" who taught him how to pray: "Since she was one of the Penitentas, I went to her when I was starting to think about joining the Hermandad."[14] He acknowledges his mother as the person who led him to join the Hermandad through her spiritual advice and guidance. His mother affirmed in him the decision to join the brotherhood at the moment that he felt ready.

In spite of the narrowly defined image of penitentes and penitentas, we find numerous stories of women who played a critical role in conveying and reinforcing the manifestations and expressions of the sacred in the Hispano communities throughout New Mexico. As early as the late nineteenth century, for example, sacred expressions were present in the lives of the early pioneers of the community of Atarque de los García, in western New Mexico. Immediately after their arrival, these pioneers began meeting in their homes on Friday evenings to pray the rosary and recognize holy days. Led by *rezadoras* and described as "early keepers of the faith," these women played a central role in all of the religious ceremonies of this community. By the early twentieth century, *rezadoras* became an integral part of Las Posadas, a Christmas celebration, and during the month of May, known as El Mes de María, they paid homage to the Mother of Jesus through celebration and religious devotion.

During the Lenten season, it was the women of Atarque who led the prayers at each station of the cross (Las Estaciones), portraying Christ's travail in his approach to Calvary. *Rezadoras,* accompanied by children, conducted religious services and taught the children to sing.[15] Lent was a season for fasting, especially for the women and teenage girls of the community.[16]

In a powerful and real way, Hispanas kept alive the religious life of this small but growing community of western New Mexico.[17] We have the stories of women leaders such as Doñas Gertrudes Ortega Chávez, Sara Landavazo Baca, and Gabrielita Martínez, who, like Hispanos throughout the Southwest, found themselves without access to a resident priest. The women of Atarque did not despair, but conducted and performed their own religious services and ceremonies. Whereas in other New Mexican communities, the Hermanos Penitentes stepped forward to keep the faith alive, it was the women of Atarque who prayed over the dying, prepared the body of the deceased, and organized all of the ceremonies for the wake and burial. During the wake, the *rezadoras* led the community in rosaries and *alabanzas* (hymns of praise), and the following day they led a procession to the *camposanto* (cemetery) for the burial. These keepers of the faith were also known to administer baptism to dying infants.[18]

The elements of practical Christianity are as important to New Mexican Hispana spirituality as they are to the brotherhood, whether or not these women are formally affiliated with the penitentes. Part of a larger communal sacred expression, women in the New Mexican sacred landscape continually work for the common good of the penitente sacred world. Like their male counterparts, women are recognized for providing spiritual advice and guidance and recreating sacred traditions. In effect, they have produced a community of memory reminding people of their unique spiritual, ethnic, gender, and regional identities.

The story of practical Christianity told by Santiago Luna at the beginning of this chapter has its female equivalent in the sacred landscape of New Mexico. Consider the role played by traditional female plasterers *(enjarradoras)* throughout New Mexican history. Through their work, women have literally had a hand in the shaping and construction of community. Universally acknowledged as work exclusively designated for women, the physical and aesthetic act of plastering is credited with the endurance of sacred structures and churches for hundreds of years in New Mexico. Historically, women have been both exterior and interior designers, plastering and protecting structures, building fireplaces *(hornos)*, and finishing floors. It is important to underscore that this form of human agency is a communal act in which both men and women contribute their knowledge and expertise toward the creation and maintenance of the New Mexican sacred landscape.[19]

In sum, the interdependence between the spiritual and material worlds described in this chapter is embodied in the lives of women and men who create and maintain Hispano Catholicism in New Mexico. Through the everyday lives of a people, practical Christianity becomes real and explicit. It transforms a penitente story into a sacred story. Like charity, prayer, and the good example, these sacred expressions acquire their meaning and understanding within the communal and material world, and in turn sacralize the history of the Hispano community in New Mexico. This style of human agency is significant because it evokes a sense of power that affirms individuals[20] by orienting them toward the collective memory of the New Mexican region and its people. The region is transformed into a *sacred place* by the *sacred sentiments* of the people.[21] The sacred as sentiment is rooted in a realm of human experiences where social relations are interdependent and emotional, and a sense of obligation is actively present. In addition, it is a place where community truly happens, produced and reproduced by memory—where women and men are actively involved in retelling its story, and in so doing, have embodied and exemplified the meaning of a community of memory. This community represents part of a "moral discourse" that transcends ahistorical individualism because remembering is inherently a social activity attached to social group membership. This is to say that all memory is structured by group identities. One remembers one's childhood as part of a family, or one's neighborhood as part of a local community.[22] This community of memory represents the spirituality imagined by Hispanos in general, and specifically, by the Hermanos Penitentes throughout New Mexican history. Penitente sacred stories and expressions were evocative words and actions that gave meaning and orientation to the Christian faith and sustained it in the place of New Mexico, and in the sentiments of its people.[23]

It is important to highlight the fact that several scholars have argued against the assumptions of spontaneity and self-reliant Hispano religious expression embedded in the notion of practical Christianity. Past scholarship asserts that Hispano and indigenous (Pueblo) sacred stories (myths), performances, rituals, and symbols embody the oppressive imprint and vestiges of the sixteenth-century Spanish colonization of New Mexico. These vestiges of Spanish hegemony have been transmitted through "conquest theater and drama," which remain in the present-day stories, rituals, and performances of Pueblo and Hispano communities.[24]

Whereas one cannot deny the fact that, in the guise of Christianity, Spanish colonization has had a profound impact on the sacred traditions of New Mexico,[25] I would argue the critical need to reassess and reinterpret historic and contemporary New Mexico and the American Southwest as a true "contact zone," as defined by Mary Louise Pratt. For Pratt, a contact zone is a "social space where disparate cultures meet, clash, and grapple with each other, often in highly asymmetrical relations of domination and subordination."[26] By incorporating this perspective, we recognize those sacred places and sacred sentiments where story (myth), performance, ritual, and symbol will at times conflict with and contradict each other, and even converge with one another, bringing forth a full range of possibilities and outcomes.[27]

Recent scholarship by Sylvia Rodríguez on the Matachines Dance in New Mexico offers us an important step in this direction. She applies the concept of the "hidden transcript" to the "conquest drama" in an attempt to explain the multiple meaning systems and expressions that have been appropriated, altered, and subtly subverted by indigenous Pueblo performers in present-day New Mexico.[28] Accordingly, it is imperative that we come to a new understanding of the penitente brotherhood in the history of New Mexico, one that interprets their sacred expressions as something more than a mere faulty imitation of official Catholicism responding to an absent or ethnocentric Catholic clergy in the region.

Instead, the contributions of the brotherhood in the New Mexican sacred world represent a practical form of Christianity that is rooted in the lived experiences and stories of a community that stand on their own merit, and in expressive styles that are characterized by popular and communal sacred expression. Over the centuries, it has enabled the brotherhood to create and sustain its own community of memory that, despite opposition from dominant forces, has given it an identity and sense of purpose in New Mexican history.[29] Penitente practical Christianity has brought to life the sacred myth of Jesus Christ through the stories and human agency of the penitente brotherhood, which over the centuries has kept the sacred alive in New Mexico and throughout the Southwest.[30]

The Story of Popular Religious Expression in Hispano/Chicano Religions

5

As a race, the people of New Mexico are extremely superstitious. . . . They have an abiding faith in saints and images, and with the mass of the inhabitants their worship
appears no more than a blind adoration of these insensitive objects. Some of the most intelligent of the better
class look upon these bits of wood as all-powerful in every
emergency.
—William W. H. Davis, *El Gringo*

You Won't Find Promised Land on most maps . . . . Perhaps that's okay, perhaps it's better Promised Land does
not appear on most maps. Maybe Promised Land lies
where it does to teach us the inadequacy of maps we
don't make ourselves, teach us how to create them,
reimagine connections others have forgotten or hidden.
Maybe we need Promised Land to be born again, 120
years after its founding, the only word on a blank page, a
word not written yet, not completely spelled out, one
around which, upon which rock will begin to inscribe a
new story.
—John Edgar Wideman, *Fatheralong*

P enitente spirituality is best understood as popular religious expression. Popular Catholicism is at the core of penitente religiosity and an indispensable feature of the larger Hispano/Chicano Roman Catholic experience in the United States. Whereas past literature identifies the prominence of popular Catholicism in the Hispano/Chicano Roman Catholic experience, I believe that it fails to provide a methodology for understanding popular religion on its own terms. The majority of past scholarship interprets popular Catholicism in relation to institutional religion.

As an alternative to this approach, I suggest the incorporation of story and storytelling as a methodology for understanding and interpreting manifestations of the sacred in the Hispano/Chicano experience. I believe that story as method provides a more complete and accurate way of understanding the sacred because it is interpreted from an experiential perspective. Emanating from the everyday experiences of Hispanos/Chicanos, popular Catholicism is best understood through a methodology that takes into account lived religious experiences.

The purpose of this book has been to tell a new and different story about the Hermanos Penitentes of New Mexico. Having analyzed and critiqued the old penitente stories of flagellation and deviance, we can replace them with stories of community, self-determination, devotion, and resilience—a story with a unique perspective into the penitente sacred world. The focus and emphasis of this new perspective is on the collective memories, historical experiences, and cultural heritage that make up this world. Beyond these dimensions, it is a world comprised of economic and political factors that also shape and give meaning to the everyday experiences, expressions, and struggles of the penitente brotherhood. Thus, within this world, the creations and constructions that guide one in knowing and understanding the sacred are found in the personal experiences and expressions of its people.[1] Story as method is at the foundation of practical Christian expressions, which explains its prominence

Penitente brother during Holy Week. Reprinted by permission from *Villages of Hispanic New Mexico*, by Nancy Hunter Warren. Photo by Nancy Hunter Warren, copyright 1987 by the School of American Research, Santa Fe.

within the penitente sacred world. It is captured throughout the penitente stories offered in this book.

Furthermore, because this perspective identifies human agency as the basis for sacred expressions within the penitente world, this approach is sensitive to the *place* where such expressions are encountered, understood, interpreted, and practiced. The actual geographical and physical space determines the ways in which an individual or community defines and interprets the sacred. This concept is extremely significant for understanding the penitente sacred world, because all penitente sacred encounters, practices, and experiences have occurred in a place outside the boundaries of institutional religion. According to the standard text on American popular religion by Peter Williams, this type of expression is defined as "popular religion" because of its external site of origin vis-à-vis established or institutional religion.[2]

Whereas Williams's definition is useful, it unfortunately limits our abilities to fully understand popular religious expression within the Hispano/Chicano Roman Catholic context. The work of Samuel Silva Gotay on popular religion in the Roman Catholic tradition focuses on popular religiosity in Puerto Rico, but it is also applicable to popular Catholicism in the penitente and Hispano/Chicano experience of the Southwest and the larger North American context. Silva Gotay emphasizes a historical and collective interpretation of the sacred in which Puerto Rican popular Catholicism "shapes a sense of collective identity" and provides people with "a sense of belonging among those who share it."[3] Like penitente and Hispano/Chicano experiences, popular Catholicism for Silva Gotay offers its followers a wellspring of strength, consolation, and, at times, even resistance to forces that seek to change it.[4] From this perspective, practical Christianity in the penitente sacred world represents popular Catholicism because it seeks to establish and preserve the collective memory and historical identity of a people.[5]

Accordingly, we discover that a significant portion of the penitente world is comprised of popular religious experiences from within the realm of Roman Catholicism. Of equal, if not greater significance for this discussion, is the fact that popular Catholicism also embodies a significant portion of the larger Hispano/Chicano religious experience. In fact, a review of the literature identifies popular religion as the central component in the Hispano/Chicano Roman Catholic experience. What we discover are categories for interpreting Hispano/Chicano popular religion that resemble the perspective put forth by Williams.

Recent literature describes popular religion in the Hispano/Chicano context as a "rereading of the doctrines and rites of the official religion" in which "alternative paths are created to circumvent the exclusive definitory power of the [religious] virtuosi."[6] Elsewhere, popular religion is interpreted as something that "falls outside of ecclesiastical control,"[7] that is "not controlled by official religious groups and their gatekeepers."[8] Furthermore, a review of past literature in Hispano/Chicano religions reveals similar interpretations. The works of McNamara, Hurtado, Murrietta, Rye, Soto, Mosqueda, Cadena, Pulido, and Thies have carved out an image of a Hispano/Chicano popular religious identity that has been shaped by larger institutional and social forces.[9]

Whereas such interpretations identify popular religion as a critical feature of the Hispano/Chicano religious experience, these conceptualizations, including the work of Williams, are heavily influenced and overshadowed by the forces of institutional religions. Popular religion is configured in response to the restrictive and oppressive nature of institutional Catholicism. Upon reflection, such a perspective makes sense when we take into account the fact that these past conceptions represent intellectual reactions and responses to the dominant and oppressive forces of institutional Catholicism that have historically been a part of the Hispano/Chicano collective experience. As a consequence, past and present discourse on the Hispano/Chicano religious experience has been shaped and molded by this perspective.

Returning to the concept of place introduced above, we extend our analysis here to include both the penitente and Hispano/Chicano sacred worlds. This notion of place offers a perspective that emphasizes the qualitative differences for interpreting sacred experiences in relation to the geographical and physical space where sacred encounters or practices occur. Consequently, a range of possibilities exists regarding how an individual will interpret their relationship to the sacred. For example, a sacred encounter within the walls of a parish church versus an encounter in the privacy of one's living room will bring forward qualitatively different accounts in terms of meaning and interpretation of the experience. Hence, I conclude that Hispano/Chicano sacred identity is directly related to the place where sacred experiences unfold. Instead of a deductive approach that creates a "structure of oppositions" by distinguishing sacred experiences as popular or institutional,[10] I prefer an inductive approach in which the location of an individual's sacred experience is emphasized.

To elaborate on this point, consider Richard R. Flores's work on the popular religious drama known as Los Pastores. This excellent study of the Mexican shepherd's play compares and contrasts performances of Los Pastores in relation to three distinct physical and geographical domains: the barrio-home, the church, and the *mission*. Flores reveals that invocation of the sacred in the barrio domain, which consists of backyards and driveways of homes, includes references to personal matters. Consider the statement made by the host of a barrio-home performance: "It has been two years since I made a vow to the Christ Child. If he cured my mother, I promised to hold a pastorela [pastoral play] in my house. Well, my mother's health improved, and I feel happy that today has arrived (Hace dos años que hice una promesa al Niño Dios. Si él curara mi mamá, yo prometería tener una pastorela en mi casa. Pues, la salud de mi mamá se mejoró, y me siento feliz que ya llegó este día)."[11] According to Flores, this manner of interpreting the sacred serves as an invitation to collective intimacy because it provides a social frame in which others are able to recall similar events in their own lives. It unites the group through a performative event common to their experiences.[12]

In contrast, performances within the church domain reveal a shift in meaning as Los Pastores is reinterpreted or "recentered." It is propagated as a cultural way of celebrating a Mexican, Roman Catholic Christmas enactment. In contrast to the barrio-home experience, the church domain experiences a shift from the familial and social to the institutional. In addition, cultural authority and knowledge of the sacred "shifts" from the hosts and performers to the priests or other Catholic officials who claim control over the event in its newly reconstituted official domain.[13]

The most salient issue regarding Flores's work in relation to the interpretation of Hispano/Chicano religions is that it has moved beyond a binary perspective that pits rigid institutional religious boundaries against more fluid manifestations of popular religious expression. Instead, he has put forth a free-standing theory for understanding the range of sacred experiences in the Hispano/Chicano world. As his work has helped clarify, the location of the sacred is critical for understanding the Hispano/Chicano community.

Accordingly, what I wish to advance as a method for understanding the Hispano/Chicano religious experience is a perspective that will allow us to get at the lived experiences and expressions of the community. My objective is to develop a methodology that will provide a more complete understanding and interpretation of the sacred in the everyday life experiences of Hispanos/Chicanos. Such a perspective is imperative, since very little is known about "religion as practiced" and the "everyday thinking and doing of lay men and women."[14] Hispano/Chicano Catholicism is a "lived religion," located in the "place where humans make something of the worlds they have found themselves thrown into."[15] Such a perspective allows scholars to understand popular Catholicism on its own terms and in its own space. In contrast, a deductive institutional perspective will silence and overshadow the complexities and range of experiences within the Hispano/Chicano world.

The forced institutionalization of penitente traditions by the Roman Catholic hierarchy silenced the range of sacred experiences within the penitente community. Interpretations of the sacred world of the penitentes were narrowly defined and restricted to acts of flagellation. Consequently, what emerged was a "flagellant-bound" historical record. It influenced the scholarly production of knowledge regarding the penitente sacred world, calling into question the reliability of the historical record in bringing forth truth and the meaning of sacredness for religious communities in American history.

A more holistic methodological approach is called for in the study of the sacred in both the penitente and Hispano/Chicano experiences. This perspective embraces story and storytelling as the central methodological approach. Through story, we incorporate both the human and insti-

Penitente services during Holy Week. Reprinted by permission from *Villages of Hispanic New Mexico,* by Nancy Hunter Warren. Photo by Nancy Hunter Warren, copyright 1987 by the School of American Research, Santa Fe.

tutional elements of an experience. The sacred is not substituted for or replaced by a collection of abstract or routinized rituals and symbols, but instead is to be understood within the Hispano experience as a whole.[16] The sacred is discovered as something real and meaningful through lived experiences and represents part of a larger sacred story or history.

Story provides us with a way to share in the penitente sacred world. By incorporating story as a methodology for the study of religion, I have sought to understand this world and, in turn, offer interpretations of penitente sacred experiences and expressions. As a result, we are left with two stories: the new penitente story, and the hidden penitente story.

The new story is the one told in this book. It constructs a penitente sacred world where a practical form of Christianity is embraced, encapsulated in the sacred triad of charity, prayer, and the good example. I have defined this sacred expression as practical Christianity, rooted in human agency within the material world.

The hidden story is the one that remains to be told.[17] It will material-
ize when a holistic methodological approach, utilizing story, is incorporated into the study of Hispano/Chicano religions. This new story will
guide us to those "hidden, secret, local, difficult to get at places"[18] in the
life experiences and expressions of the Hispano/Chicano community—
those places within everyday life where the sacred is encountered, practiced, understood, and interpreted. Borrowing from the quote by John
Edgar Wideman with which this chapter began, it is imperative that
scholars of Hispano/Chicano religions begin to tell their own stories
about "Promised Lands."

Notes

Preface

1. Sabine R. Ulibarrí, "Brujerías o Tonterías?" in *Mi abuela fumaba puros y otros cuentos de Tierra Amarilla* (Berkeley: Quinto Sol, 1977), 55.

2. Throughout this book, the terms *Hispano* and *Chicano* are used to encompass both genders: Hispana/Hispano and Chicana/Chicano.

3. Feliciano Rivera, *A Mexican American Source Book* (Menlo Park: Educational Consulting Associates, 1970).

4. See Kirin Narayan, *Storytellers, Saints, and Scoundrels: Folk Narrative in Hindu Religious Teaching* (Philadelphia: University of Pennsylvania Press, 1989), 243.

5. See Stephen Crites, "Angels We Have Heard," in *Religion as Story,* ed. James B. Wiggins (New York: Harper and Row, 1975), 26; Leslie Marmon Silko, *Ceremony* (New York: Penguin, 1977); and *Storyteller* (New York: Arcade, 1981); "Conversations with Leslie Marmon Silko," *Suntracks* 3 (1976): 28–33; and James L. Peacock, "Society as Narrative," in *Forms of Symbolic Action,* ed. Robert F. Spencer (Seattle: American Ethnological Society, 1969), 167–78.

6. Stephen Crites, "The Narrative Quality of Experience," *Journal of the Academy of Religion* 39 (1971): 295.

7. Wendy Doniger O'Flaherty, *Other People's Myths: The Cave of Echoes* (Chicago: University of Chicago Press, 1995), 4.

8. See Crites, "Narrative Quality of Experience," 291–311; Tomás Rivera, "Chicano Literature: Fiesta of the Living," in *The Identification and Analysis of Chicano Literature,* ed. Francisco Jiménez (New York: Bilingual Press, 1979).

9. Within the field of Chicano studies, this perspective has been described as the "historical dialectical approach" by Joseph Sommers and "autobioethnography" by Norma Elia Cantú. See Joseph Sommers, "Critical Approaches to Chicano Literature," in *Modern Chicano Writers: A Collection of Critical Essays,* ed. Joseph Sommers and Tomás Ybarra-Frausto (Engelwood: Prentice Hall,

1979), 36; and Norma Elia Cantú, *Canícula: Snapshots of a Girlhood en la Frontera* (Albuquerque: University of New Mexico Press, 1995), 1.

10. See Crites, "Narrative Quality of Experience," 295.

11. Narayan, *Storytellers*, 244.

12. The term *Hispano* is used in this study specifically to describe the subgroup of Mexicanos or, subsequently, Mexican Americans/Chicanos who settled in the Upper Rio Grande and adjacent regions of northern Mexico and southern Colorado. See Sylvia Rodríguez, "Land, Water, and Ethnic Identity in Taos," in *Land, Water, and Culture: New Perspectives on Hispanic Land Grants*, ed. Charles L. Briggs and John R. Van Ness (Albuquerque: University of New Mexico Press, 1987), 313–403.

13. Clay Thompson, "Charity not Zealotry," *Arizona Republic*, August 29, 1998, D6.

14. Maxine Hong Kingston, "A Song for a Barbarian Reed Pipe," in *The Woman Warrior: Memoirs of a Girlhood among Ghosts* (New York: Vintage, 1976), 216.

15. Garrett Hongo, as quoted in *Where the Body Meets Memory: An Odyssey of Race, Sexuality and Identity*, by David Mura (New York: Anchor, 1996), 19.

Introduction

1. Carl N. Taylor, *Odyssey of the Islands* (New York: Charles Scribner's Sons, 1936).

2. Katherine Woods, "In the Jungles of the Philippines: The Adventures of Carl Taylor among the Pygmy Head-Hunters and the Tree-Travelers of the Islands," *New York Times Book Review*, July 19, 1936, 5.

3. Ibid.

4. "Was Warned of Houseboy by Woman Friend," *Albuquerque Journal*, February 7, 1936.

5. "Cries in Cell after Sentence," *Albuquerque Journal*, February 18, 1936, 2.

6. Carl N. Taylor, "Agony in New Mexico," *Today*, February 15, 1936, 3.

7. Ibid.

8. Ibid.

9. I draw from Paul Fussell's work on travel writing for this definition of vagabond narratives. In particular, see Paul Fussell, *Abroad: British Literary Traveling between the Wars* (New York: Oxford, 1980).

10. Roy De S. Horn believed that Taylor was possibly the victim of some "strange penitente plot" because of three photographs allegedly taken inside of the local penitente *morada* by Taylor. Raymond Moley quoted from Taylor's *Agony in New Mexico*, in which Taylor expressed his belief that the young Trujillo was a member of the penitente brotherhood. See "Boy, 15, Faces Death

for Murdering Taylor," *Albuquerque Journal,* February 7, 1936; and Taylor, "Agony in New Mexico," 3–4, 20–21.

11. According to Marta Weigle, the Taylor murder was a "windfall for the pulps and the papers." See *Brothers of Light, Brothers of Blood: The Penitentes of the Southwest* (Santa Fe: Ancient City Press, 1976), 108.

12. Beginning in 1936 and continuing into 1937, newspapers and magazines throughout the United States took notice of the penitentes and ran feature stories and series that scandalized the brotherhood in an attempt to link so-called penitente practices to the killing of Carl Taylor. In addition, an hour-long film was produced in 1936 that provided a fictional account of the murder, claiming that Trujillo had been influenced by the penitentes, in an attempt to establish a connection between the penitentes and the killing.

13. The most recognized accounts of the penitentes include Josiah Gregg, *Commerce of the Prairies* (Philadelphia: J. B. Lippincott, 1962); Charles F. Lummis, *The Land of Poco Tiempo* (New York: C. Scribner's Son, 1893); Alice Corbin Henderson, *Brothers of Light: The Penitentes of the Southwest* (New York: Harcourt, Brace, 1937); Alexander M. Darley, *The Passionists of the Southwest* (Glorieta, N.M.: Rio Grande Press, 1968); Fray Angélico Chávez, "The Penitentes of New Mexico," *New Mexico Historical Review* 29 (1954): 97–123; Dorothy Woodward, *The Penitentes of New Mexico* (New York: Arno Press, 1974); E. Boyd, "The Third Order of St. Francis and the Penitentes of New Mexico," in *Popular Arts of Spanish Mexico* (Santa Fe: Museum of New Mexico Press, 1974); and Weigle, *Brothers of Light.* More recent publications include Thomas J. Steele and S. J. and Rowena A. Rivera, *Penitente Self-Government: Brotherhoods and Councils, 1797–1947* (Santa Fe: Ancient City Press, 1985); and William Wroth, *Images of Penance, Images of Mercy: Southwestern Santos in the Late Nineteenth Century* (Norman: University of Oklahoma Press, 1991). The flagellant image of the penitente is still prevalent in the recent literature. See Ray John de Aragon, *Hermanos de la Luz: Brothers of the Light* (Santa Fe: Heartsfire Books, 1998). Marta Weigle's definitive study of the penitentes is the most recognized exception to sensationalized scholarship focusing on the brotherhood and has set the standard for future penitente scholarship. Weigle accurately acknowledges that most penitente scholarship focuses on the "spectacular" and "sensationalistic" aspects of the brotherhood and overlooks the benefits of this religious community. According to Weigle, besides herself, Woodward, Chávez, and Boyd have written the most accurate studies of the penitentes. She, like Chávez and Boyd,

drew from the archives of the Archdiocese of Santa Fe. Building on the work of Woodward, Chávez, and Boyd, she was the first to draw as well from the Spanish, Mexican, and territorial archives of New Mexico. For a complete review of the literature on the penitentes through 1976, see Marta Weigle, *A Penitente Bibliography* (Albuquerque: University of New Mexico Press, 1976).

14. Weigle, *Brothers of Light,* chapters 7 and 8.

15. Mircea Eliade, *The Sacred and the Profane* (New York: Harcourt Brace Jovanovich, 1959). The notion of great powers, related to my definition of sacred stories, is discussed fully in the preface.

16. This interpretation of the sacred draws from the works of Mircea Eliade and Charles Long. See Mircea Eliade, *Ordeal by Labyrinth* (Chicago: University of Chicago Press, 1982); and Charles H. Long, *Significations: Signs, Symbols, and Images in the Interpretation of Religion* (Philadelphia: Fortress, 1986).

17. Davíd Carrasco, "A Perspective for a Study of Religious Dimensions in Chicano Experience: *Bless Me, Ultima* as a Religious Text." *Aztlán* 13, nos. 1 and 2 (1982): 206–7.

18. Long, *Significations,* 7.

19. See Wendy Doniger O'Flaherty, *Other People's Myths: The Cave of Echoes* (Chicago: University of Chicago Press, 1988).

20. This is drawn directly from the work of Richard Bauman, who refers to storytelling as "oral literature" and asserts that it has its primary existence in the action of people and their roots in social and cultural life. Richard Bauman, *Story, Performance, and Event: Contextual Studies of Oral Narrative* (New York: Cambridge University Press, 1993), 1–2.

21. Since 1990, two national organizations have emerged over the past ten years for the study of Chicano and Latino religions: the Program for the Analysis of Religions for the Study of Latinos (PARAL), and the National Association for the Study of Chicano Religions (NASCR). There now exists a significant body of literature in the field, which is discussed briefly in chapter 5.

22. This *hermano* prefers not to be named.

Chapter 1. Haciendo Penitencia

1. Candy Martinez, personal interview, July 19, 1994.

2. Ibid.

3. In one of the many collections of stories of the Río Puerco Valley by Nasario García, we are introduced to the stories of Teodorita García-Ruelas and Adelita Gonzáles. Both of these stories speak to the mutual and reciprocal re-

lations established among neighbors in New Mexican communities. Teodorita García-Ruelas, "Baile y baile y sin harina!"; and Adelita Gonzales, "Dios nos tenía bendecidos con la comida que teníanos," in *Abuelitos: Stories of the Río Puerco Valley*, ed. Nasario García (Albuquerque: University of New Mexico Press, 1992), 99, 125. Also see the unpublished files of the WPA, which document numerous acts of mutuality and reciprocity, in particular, "Tía Lupe" and "Some of Tía Lupe's Contemporaries: Stories of Some New Mexico Grandmothers," File 17, Folkways, New Mexico State Records and Archives; and Cleo Jaramillo, *Romance of a Little Village Girl* (San Antonio: Naylor, 1955), 36–37.

4. Penitente brother, personal interview, August 12, 1993. Also see Jo Roybal Izay, "La Cofradía de los Nazarenos," *El Hispano* 23, no. 45 (March 29, 1989): 3.

5. Robert Sprott, *Making Up What Is Lacking: Towards an Interpretation of the Penitentes,* Working Paper 110 (Southwest Hispanic Research Center, University of New Mexico, 1984), 3.

6. Alberto L. Pulido, "The Religious Dimension of Mexican Americans," in *The History of the Mexican American People,* ed. Julian Samora (Notre Dame: University of Notre Dame Press, 1993), 225.

7. Moises Sandoval, *On the Move: A History of the Hispanic Church in the United States* (New York: Orbis, 1990), 21–22.

8. Alberto L. Pulido, "Mexican American Catholicism in the Southwest: The Transformation of a Popular Religion," *Perspectives in Mexican American Studies* 4 (1993): 93–108.

9. Penitente brother, personal interview, August 12, 1993.

10. Penitente brother, telephone interview, February 23, 1997.

11. The perspective taken in this book represents a significant departure from past penitente studies, which focus on negative aspects of penance such as the flagellant practices of the brotherhood and ignore the spiritual and religious character of the penitente brotherhood. See, for example, Lorayne Ann Horka-Follock, *Los Hermanos Penitentes: A Vestige of Medievalism in Southwestern United States* (Tucson: Westernlore, 1987), 53, 112.

12. Penitente brother, personal interview, August 12, 1993. Also see a brother's vignette in *En Divina Luz: The Penitente Moradas of New Mexico,* by Craig Varjabedian and Michael Wallis (Albuquerque: University of New Mexico Press, 1994), 22. The noun *doing* is translated literally from the Spanish *haciendo,* which is from the verb *hacer,* which means "to do" or "to make." *Doing* is used in this book to describe an act, action, or performance by a group or indi-

vidual. Therefore, *haciendo oración* literally means "doing prayer," or "praying." In this study, prayer in the penitente sacred world represents an act or action. This idea of "prayer as agency" is fully developed in chapter 4.

13. Penitente brother, telephone interview, April 17, 1997.

14. Weigle, *Brothers of Light,* 162–66.

15. Penitente brother, telephone interview, April 17, 1997.

16. Penitente brother, as quoted in Varjabedian and Wallis, *En Divina Luz,* 22–23.

17. Sam Gill, *Native American Religious Action: A Performance Approach to Religion* (Columbia: University of South Carolina Press, 1987), 89–112. It is important to note that Gill borrows from the Zuni, who differentiate between "prayer as text" and "prayer as act."

18. Penitente brother, personal interview, August 12, 1993.

19. Ibid.

20. Ibid.

21. The narrative is comprised of three lengthy personal interviews, conducted with Hermano Luna on July 1, 1997; March 31, 1998; and July 26, 1998.

22. For historical information on Los Ojitos and Puerto de Luna, see F. Stanley, "The Puerto de Luna New Mexico Story," manuscript, Nazareth, Texas, December 1969; A. J. Padilla, "My Manuscript," manuscript, Puerto de Luna, New Mexico, 1958; and Otto Goetz, "Santa Rosa, New Mexico," *New Mexico Historical Review* 23, no. 3 (July 1948): 165–76.

23. This is an English translation of the popular and enduring *alabado* that begins this section. Hermano Luna identified it as the most powerful and memorable *alabado* of his life.

24. This image of the "redeeming values of the cross" is a significant dimension of "penitente theology" and, according to one brother, is associated with the biblical scripture of Moses lifting the bronze serpent in the desert. See C. Gilbert Romero, "Teología de las raices de un pueblo: Los penitentes de Nuevo Mexico," *Servir* 83–84 (1979): 625–26.

25. Santiago Luna, personal interview, July 1, 1997.

Chapter 2. Risking It All for Civilization

1. "Boy, 15, Faces Death for Murdering Taylor," *Albuquerque Journal,* February 7, 1936, 2.

2. Ibid. It is important to note that none of these photographs were ever published.

3. Some newspapers chose to restrict their coverage solely to the Taylor mur-

NOTES TO PAGES 26–27   87

der. In addition to the regional coverage in the *Albuquerque Journal* and the *Santa Fe New Mexican,* restricted coverage of the murder appeared in nationally distributed periodicals, including the *Chicago Daily Tribune,* the *New York Times,* the *San Francisco Chronicle,* and the *Tucson Daily Citizen.* However, the *San Francisco Chronicle* and the *Tucson Daily Citizen* eventually ran scandalous stories about the penitente brotherhood.

4. "Brutal Murder of Wandering Writer Unveils Weird New Mexico Torture Cult Rites He Was about to Expose," *Cleveland News,* February 8, 1936, 1.

5. "Blood in New Mexico," *Time,* March 9, 1936, 36.

6. "Slaying of Author Bares Secret Worship Rites of Strange Mountain Cult," *Cleveland News,* February 7, 1936, 1.

7. Ibid.

8. "Penitentes' Vengeance for Expose Blamed in Taylor Death," *Los Angeles Examiner,* February 8, 1936, 1.

9. George Mills and Richard Groves, in their study *Lucifer and the Crucifer: The Enigma of the Penitentes* (Denver: Brand Books, 1955, 5–7), devised a system for classifying eyewitness accounts of penitente behavior. All first-hand eyewitness accounts, the most reliable, were defined as Class I, and anonymous second-hand eyewitness accounts as Class II. The more a Class II account was in line with a Class I account, the more reliable it became. Interestingly enough, a Class II account became supportable when it had been repeated so often in Class I accounts that it was considered to be true. According to the authors, the Class I–Class II dichotomy was established to challenge and move away from the "salivate-at-the-sight-of-blood school of thought."

10. "Desert Golgotha: Penitentes Reenact Christ's Passion with Actual Crucifixion," *Literary Digest,* April 3, 1937, 31. Also see Marcus Bach, "Crucifixion by Request," *Christian Century,* March 10, 1937, which "Desert Golgotha" draws from rather heavily. Bach described the *hermano mayor* as a "dictator" in civic and religious affairs. This perspective is also found in Horka-Follick, *Hermanos Penitentes,* 99.

11. "Queer Religious Cult, Strange Rites in New Mexico: Slaying Linked to Penitentes," *San Francisco Chronicle,* February 11, 1936, 4.

12. Ibid.

13. In the second article of the series, it was stated that "membership of the Penitentes is limited to members of the Catholic church and are mainly Spanish Americans, although it is reported, a few white Americans have obtained membership for political reasons." "Burial Alive Is Penalty, Weird Cult

Guards Rules: Procession Members Flogged," *San Francisco Chronicle*, February 12, 1936, 2.

14. George Kennedy, "Boy's Confession in Killing of Writer Fails to Calm Cult Vengeance," *New York American*, March 1, 1936.

15. "Horror Told by Cameraman," *Los Angeles Examiner*, February 8, 1936, 3.

16. *Lash of the Penitentes*, directed by Mike J. Levinson, 1936 (abridged version).

17. "Yellow Journalism," *Santa Fe New Mexican*, February 14, 1936, 4.

18. Weigle, *Brothers of Light*, 108.

19. Bach, "Crucifixion."

20. Mabel De La Mater Scacheri, "The Penitentes: Murderous or Misguided?" *Family Circle*, March 20, 1936, 15.

21. Ibid.

22. Paul Horgan, *Josiah Gregg and His Vision of the Early West* (New York: Farrar Straus Giroux, 1979), 17–18, 29.

23. Gregg, *Commerce*, vii.

24. Ibid.

25. Horgan, *Josiah Gregg*, 31.

26. Ibid., 10.

27. Ibid., 29.

28. Ibid., 29–30.

29. Gregg, *Commerce*, 137.

30. Ibid., 138.

31. Ibid.

32. Ibid.

33. For example, Edwin T. Randall referred to Charles Lummis as the "great authority" of the penitentes. "Penitent Americans Torture Themselves," *Cleveland Plain Dealer*, Magazine Section, March 15, 1936, 1.

34. Charles F. Lummis, *The Land of Poco Tiempo* (Albuquerque: University of New Mexico, 1952), 61.

35. Lummis, *Land of Poco Tiempo*, 64.

36. Ibid., 66.

37. Ibid., 75.

38. David Roberts, "A Tough Little Guy Became the Original Southwest Booster," *Smithsonian* 21, no. 2 (May 1990) : 117–18.

39. Ibid., 118.

40. "An Apostle of the Southwest," *New York Times*, November 27, 1928, 2. Else-

where, Lummis was identified as the founder of the "southwest genre," a man who had tremendous impact because both professionals and the popular media recognized him as the "undisputed authority of the history, anthropology, and folklore of the southwest." *Criticism in the Borderlands: Studies in Chicano Literature, Culture and Ideology*, ed. Hector Calderón and José David Saldívar (Durham: Duke University Press, 1991), 3.

41. Leah Dilworth, *Imagining Indians in the Southwest: Persistent Visions of a Primitive Past* (Washington, D.C.: Smithsonian Institution Press, 1996).

42. Abigail A. Van Slyck, "Mañana, Mañana: Racial Stereotypes and the Anglo Rediscovery of the Southwest's Vernacular Architecture, 1890–1920," in *Gender, Class, and Shelter*, ed. Elizabeth Collins Cromely and Carter L. Hudgins (Knoxville: University of Tennessee Press, 1995): 97.

43. With the introduction of the railroad, the Southwest was transformed into a major tourist and commercial attraction and art colony. Artists were hired by the Atchison, Topeka, and Santa Fe Railroad with this specific goal in mind. See Ted Schwarz, "The Santa Fe Railway and Early Southwest Artists," *American West* (September–October 1982): 32–41; Marta Weigle, "Exposition and Mediation: Mary Colter, Erna Fergusson, and the Santa Fe/Harvey Popularization of the Native Southwest, 1902–1940," *Frontiers* 12, no. 3 (1992): 116–50; and Sylvia Rodríguez, "Art, Tourism, and Race Relations in Taos: Toward a Sociology of the Art Colony," *Journal of Anthropological Research* 45 (spring 1989): 77–99.

44. Charles F. Lummis, "The Southwestern Wonderland: An American Passion-Play," *Land of Sunshine* 4, no. 6 (May 1896): 255–56. It is important to note that Lummis's thesis correlating the demise of the brotherhood with the advent of technology and American civilization would be challenged directly by the work of Laurence F. Lee. Originally written as a undergraduate thesis in 1910, Lee's work appeared in published form ten years later in *El Palacio*. This article would reignite the debate surrounding penitente and Hispano cultural remnants in twentieth-century America. Laurence F. Lee, "Los Hermanos Penitentes," *El Palacio* 8, no. 1 (January 31, 1920): 3–20.

45. T. J. Jackson Lears, *No Place of Grace* (New York: Pantheon, 1981); Van Slyck, "Mañana."

46. Michael Heisley, "Lummis and Mexican-American Folklore," in *Chas F. Lummis: The Centennial Exhibition: Commemorating His Tramp across the Continent*, ed. Daniela P. Moneta (Los Angeles: Southwest Museum, 1985), 60–68.

Chapter 3. Storytelling, Sacredness, Truth, and Power

1. Frances Margaret Campbell, "American Catholicism in Northern New Mexico: A Kaleidoscope of Development, 1840–1885" (Ph.D. diss., Graduate Theological Union, 1986), 233.

2. The one marked difference was that this was the first episcopal visit by a bishop of Durango to New Mexico as a Mexican territory, and the first in over seventy years since Bishop Pedro Tamarón y Romeral's visit in 1760, when it was a Spanish territory.

3. Campbell, "American Catholicism," 51.

4. Ibid.

5. Fray Angélico Chávez, *My Penitente Land: Reflections on Spanish New Mexico* (Santa Fe: Museum of New Mexico Press, 1993), 235–36.

6. Ibid.; Chávez, "Penitentes of New Mexico," 110–11; Weigle, *Brothers of Light,* 242–43.

7. Chávez, "Penitentes of New Mexico," 111.

8. Chávez, *My Penitente Land,* 236–37. At the crux of Bishop Zubiría's opposition was public flagellation organized by societies. According to Chávez, the bishop could not condemn private flagellation because it was routinely practiced in monasteries under the discreet guidance of a spiritual director.

9. According to Marta Weigle, Lamy apparently approved rules for penitentes as early as February 17, 1853, which are no longer available. This document may have resembled the constitution, reprinted in translation by Alexander Darley and Dorothy Woodward, and consisting of ten articles that describe the duties of the officers, certain prayers and meditations, and indications of proper penitential practices. Weigle, *Brothers of Light,* 53–54.

10. The narrative is based on Rule 9, given here in its entirety: "All and every one of the individuals of the brotherhood shall obey and respect the legitimate Supreme pastor of this territory, His Grace, the Most Reverend Catholic Bishop, Juan Lamy and his successors in all matters which he may be pleased to ordain, whether it be this or any other matter and likewise in the same manner the parish priest, whom he many be pleased to place in this or any other point of his diocese without complaining or grumbling regarding dispositions of these matters which the prelate may be pleased to ordain and anyone who having been duly advised should insist in so doing he shall be expelled from the brotherhood as unworthy of being a member of a Catholic congregation, the fundamental basis of which is obedience and charity." Weigle, *Brothers of Light,* 203.

11. This is based on Rule 10, of which the most important section follows: "It shall be the duty of the president (Hermano Mayor) to deliver to the parish priest a list of all the persons who may belong to the brotherhood so that he may be at all times able to answer as to the conduct of each of the individuals and thus foresee the slander that may be committed by some ill intentioned members in the name of the brotherhood." Weigle, *Brothers of Light*, 203.

12. Weigle, *Brothers of Light*, 54. Five more rules were instituted by Bishop Lamy on March 9, 1857, which worked toward syncretizing the institutional church with penitente tradition. According to these rules, all brothers were required to make their confession before doing acts of penance, all acts of penance were to be conducted in hiding and seclusion without scandal, and all brothers were imposed a tax of two *reales* for wax. Weigle, *Brothers of Light*, 205–6. Also see the work of Campbell, who offers a useful discussion of these syncretizing actions by Bishop Lamy toward Hispano popular tradition, which she refers to as "doubling." "American Catholicism," 206–18.

13. Weigle, *Brothers of Light*, 207.

14. Ibid., 56, 207.

15. Ibid., 55–57.

16. Fray Angélico Chávez, *But Time and Chance: The Story of Padre Martínez of Taos, 1793–1867* (Santa Fe: Sunstone Press, 1981), 35; Chávez, *My Penitente Land,* 108.

17. Chávez, "Penitentes of New Mexico," 97–98.

18. Ibid.

19. Campbell, "American Catholicism," 70.

20. Ibid.

21. Ibid., 78.

22. Ibid., 71–74.

23. Ibid., 74, 79.

24. Juan Romero, *Reluctant Dawn: Historia del Padre A. J. Martínez, Cura de Taos* (San Antonio: Mexican American Cultural Center, 1976); Chávez, *But Time and Chance;* Thomas J. Steele, *New Mexican Spanish Religious Oratory, 1800–1900* (Albuquerque: University of New Mexico Press, 1997), chapter 2.

25. Romero, *Reluctant Dawn,* 28.

26. New Mexicans in general were opposed to tithing on practical grounds that had little to do with the spiritual authority of the church. They argued that this money just served to enrich the collectors and did not remain in the province. David J. Weber, *The Mexican Frontier, 1821–1846: The American*

Southwest under Mexico (Albuquerque: University of New Mexico Press, 1982), 75.

27. Romero, *Reluctant Dawn,* 29.

28. Ibid., 30.

29. Ibid., 31–32.

30. Much has been written about Padre Martínez's relationship to and role with the penitente brotherhood of New Mexico. William Wroth addresses the fact that Padre Martínez went from first wishing to censure public penitence in 1833 to becoming the chief advocate of the brothers by 1851, if not earlier. He documents a letter from Padre Martínez to Bishop Zubiría dated February 21, 1833. Wroth argues that this change came about as a result of the American occupation of 1846. Changes in sovereignty with the introduction of foreign cultures symbolically transformed the penitente brotherhood into the preservers of traditional Hispano spirituality. This symbolic role of the brotherhood could also be extended to the native New Mexican clergy and explain the conflicts between the native clergy and the French/American hierarchy. Wroth, *Images of Penance,* 51–52.

31. Rev. James H. Defouri, *Historical Sketch of the Catholic Church in New Mexico* (San Francisco: McCormick Brothers, 1887), 142.

32. Weigle, *Brothers of Light,* 57.

33. Francis Leon Swadesh, *Los Primeros Pobladores: Hispanic Americans of the Ute Frontier* (Notre Dame: University of Notre Dame Press, 1974), 76. Chávez states, "We may assume that Lamy tried at first to abolish the Penitentes and failed." "Penitentes of New Mexico," 99.

34. Weigle, *Brothers of Light,* 57, 251.

35. Ibid., 58–59.

36. Ibid., 207–8.

37. Ibid.

38. Chávez, "Penitentes of New Mexico," 100.

39. Weigle, *Brothers of Light,* 60.

40. Ibid., 211–16.

41. Campbell, "American Catholicism," chapter 2.

42. For additional information on Roman Catholicism, see Timothy Matovina, *Tejano Religion and Ethnicity: San Antonio, 1821–1860* (Austin: University of Texas, 1995); and Pulido, "Mexican American Catholicism," 93–108. On Protestantism, see Darley, *Passionists;* and Susan M. Yohn, *A Contest of Faiths:*

Missionary Women and Pluralism in the American Southwest (Ithaca: Cornell University Press, 1995), chapter 4.

43. Through the work of Don Miguel Archibeque, among others, Archbishop Byrne signed an official statement recognizing the Brothers of Jesus of Nazareth on January 28, 1947. A year earlier, the official Archbishop's Supreme Council had been formed to direct the several district councils, with Hermano Archibeque appointed as the first *hermano supremo arzobispal*. Weigle, *Brothers of Light*, 110–112. Also see Charles Aranda, *The Penitente Papers*, self-published, Albuquerque, 1984; "Penitentes to Get Blessing, Says Archbishop," *Albuquerque Journal*, January 31, 1947; and "Milder Forms of Penance Replace Penitente Rites," *Albuquerque Journal*, March 23, 1951.

44. Chávez, "Penitentes of New Mexico"; Weigle, *Brothers of Light*. I use the concept of "scholarship" rather loosely here, considering the range of writers and self-professed experts on penitente traditions who have documented their story. My perspective is more in line with the quote by Sam Gill that opens this chapter.

45. Gregg, *Commerce*, 134.

46. Darley, *Passionists*.

47. Lummis, *Land of Poco Tiempo*, 61.

48. Randi Jones Walker, *Protestantism in the Sangre de Cristos, 1850–1920* (Albuquerque: University of New Mexico Press, 1991), 18.

49. Rev. William E. Barton, *The Penitentes of New Mexico* (Boston: Congregational Education Society, n.d.), 8.

50. J. Manuel Espinosa, "The Origin of the Penitentes of New Mexico: Separating Fact from Fiction." *Catholic Historical Review* 79, no. 3 (1993): 454, 460.

51. Wroth, *Images of Penance*, 46–50; Espinosa, 471–76.

52. Wroth, *Images of Penance*, 45–46.

53. Chávez, "Penitentes of New Mexico," 108–14; Espinosa, "Origin," 464–71.

54. Chávez, "Penitentes of New Mexico," 114.

55. Espinosa, "Origin," 462.

56. Ibid.

57. Ibid., 463.

58. Ibid., 477.

59. Henderson, *Brothers of Light*, 10.

60. Andrew Gulliford, "Folklore in the Southwest: From Los Penitentes to Pysanka," *Journal of the Southwest* 32, no. 2 (summer 1990): 206.

61. Horka-Follick, *Hermanos Penitentes*, 4.
62. Henderson, *Brothers of Light*, 10.
63. It is important to highlight that a handful of penitente studies emphasize the social, communal, and cultural role of the brotherhood in communities throughout the Southwest. Besides the work of Marta Weigle, extremely perceptive work has been done by Romero, "Teología," 609–30. Also see Janie Louise Aragón, "The Cofradías of New Mexico: A Proposal and a Periodization," *Aztlán* 9 (1978): 101–18; Paul Kutsche and Dennis Gallegos, "Community Functions of the Cofradía de Nuestro Padre Jesús Nazareno," in *The Survival of Spanish American Villages*, ed. Paul Kutsche (Colorado Springs: R & K, 1979), 91–98; José Amaro Hernández, *Mutual Aid for Survival: The Case of the Mexican American* (Florida: Krieger Publishing, 1983); and Marta Weigle and Thomas R. Lyons, "Brothers and Neighbors: The Celebration of Community in Penitente Villages," in *Celebration: Studies in Festivity and Ritual*, ed. Victor Turner (Washington, D.C.: Smithsonian Institution Press, 1982), 231–51.
64. See, for example, his description of the personal penitential practices of Fray Francisco de Jesús María Casañas. Espinosa, "Origin," 461–62.
65. See Weigle, *Brothers of Light*, 215.
66. Wroth, *Images of Penance*, 17; Weigle, *Brothers of Light*, 187–89.
67. Ramón A. Gutiérrez, "Crucifixion, Slavery, and Death: The Hermanos Penitentes of the Southwest," in *Over the Edge: Remapping the American West*, ed. Valerie J. Matsumoto and Blake Allmendinger (Berkeley: University of California, 1999), 255–56; and "The Hermanos Penitentes: Their Altars, Their History," *Spirit*, fall–winter 1995–96, 6–13.
68. de Aragon, *Hermanos*, vii.
69. Sprott, "Making Up What Is Lacking," 7.

Chapter 4. The Story of Penitente Spirituality as Practical Christianity

1. Santiago Luna, personal interview, June 26, 1998.
2. This is a modified version of Inga Clendinnen's notion of "religion as performed" perspective. "Ways to the Sacred: Reconstructing 'Religion' in Sixteenth Century Mexico," *History and Anthropology* 5 (1990): 110–11. Also see Gill, *Native American Religious Action*, 152–53.
3. It is characterized as a sacrifice because one "has to go out of their way to do it."
4. Weigle, *Brothers of Light*, 144.

5. Jo Roybal Izay, "Los Penitentes," *El Hispano,* March 30, 1990, 3.

6. Weigle, *Brothers of Light,* 146.

7. Ibid., 145.

8. de Aragon, *Hermanos,* 38.

9. Ibid., 36, 76.

10. This story was told by the daughter of Señora Córdova, Jesusita Aragón, in de Aragon, *Hermanos,* 38–39.

11. New Mexico WPA Writer's Project entry from J. B. Cisneros, as cited in Weigle, *Brothers of Light,* 144.

12. Weigle, *Brothers of Light,* 145. It is interesting that the Beatas are said to have practiced a more "severe penance" than their male counterparts, and their oath to the group was said to be "more rigorous." Roybal Izay, "Los Penitentes," 3.

13. Penitente brother, as quoted in Varjabedian and Wallis, *En Divina Luz,* 20.

14. Ibid.

15. Pauline Chávez Bent, *Atarque: Now All Is Silent,* self-published, 1993, 6; and "The Faith, Courage, and Spirit of New Mexico's Hispanic Pioneering Women: A Profile of Rural Catholicism," in *Seeds of Struggle, Harvest of Faith: The Papers of the Archdiocese of Santa Fe Catholic Cuarto Centennial Conference on the History of the Catholic Church in New Mexico,* ed. Thomas J. Steele, Paul Rhetts, and Barbe Await (Albuquerque: LPD Press, 1998), 311–29.

16. As told in *Atarque,* by Pauline Chávez Bent, "To my recollection, no man or boy fasted" (15).

17. According to U.S. Census figures, there were 30 people in Atarque in 1885 and 304 in 1920. I wish to thank Pauline Chávez Bent for locating and sharing this information with me.

18. Chávez Bent, "Faith, Courage, and Spirit," 315–18.

19. See Sarah Deutsch, *No Separate Refuge: Culture, Class and Gender on an Anglo-Hispanic Frontier in the American Southwest, 1880–1940* (New York: Oxford University Press), 54; "Anita Rodríguez: Mother of Earth, Mistress of Mud," *New Mexico Designer/Builder,* July–August, 1994; Lorin W. Brown, "Jesu' Cristo a Caballo," in *Women of New Mexico: Depression Era Images,* ed. Marta Weigle (Santa Fe: Ancient City Press, 1993), 12.

20. See Cheryl Townsend Gilkes, "Together and in Harness: Women's Traditions in the Sanctified Church," *Signs: Journal of Women in Culture and Society* 10, no. 41 (1985): 337–98.

21. The concept of the sacred as sentiment is adapted from the work of Thomas

Bender, *Community and Social Change in America* (Baltimore: Johns Hopkins University Press, 1991), 10.

22. Robert Bellah, Richard Madsen, William M. Sullivan, Ann Swindler, and Steven Tipton, *Habits of the Heart: Individualism and Commitment in American Life* (New York: Harper and Row, 1985), 153.

23. Sprott, "Making Up What Is Lacking," 17–18.

24. Ramón Gutiérrez, "The Politics of Theater in Colonial New Mexico: Drama and the Rhetoric of Conquest," in *Reconstructing a Chicano/a Literary Heritage: Hispanic Colonial Literature of the Southwest,* ed. María Herrera-Sobek (Tucson: University of Arizona Press, 1993), 49–67. Also see Richard C. Trexler, "We Think, They Act: Clerical Readings of Missionary Theater in Sixteenth Century New Spain," in *Understanding Popular Culture: Europe from the Middle Ages to the Nineteenth Century,* ed. Steven L. Kaplan (Berlin: Mouton Publishing, 1984), 189–227; and Robert Ricard, *The Spiritual Conquest of Mexico* (Berkeley: University of California Press, 1966), chapter 12. It is very interesting that early twentieth-century interpretations of penitente Lenten rituals were characterized as "American Passion Plays." This idea was first introduced by the American novelist Mary Austin, who offered a mystical and empathetic account of Lenten penitente rites. Mary Austin, "The Trail of the Blood: An Account of the Penitent Brotherhood of New Mexico," *Century* 86 (1924): 35–44. The passion play framework would be embraced by future writers, minus the empathy. See Earle R. Forrest, "The Sanguinary Passion Play of the Penitentes," *Travel,* December 1927, 29–32, 48.

25. Without a doubt, traces of Franciscanism and Franciscan tradition are evident throughout penitente sacred expressions. The ideals of St. Francis of Assisi exist throughout the manifestations of penitente practical Christianity, along with charity, prayer, and the good example. Consider the work of Hilarin Felder, who instructs us that in Franciscanism, the act of loving humankind "by very necessity" reflects an "extraordinary love of God," exhibited through a Franciscan's willingness to obey one another in the "spirit of charity"—a spirit that is ideally an "active practical charity." Hilarin Felder, *The Ideals of St. Francis of Assisi* (Chicago: Franciscan Herald Press, 1982), 243–44, 264. Also see Sprott, "Making Up What Is Lacking," 18–25. This topic, incorporated with the impact of "conquest dramas" on the communities of northern New Spain, northern Mexico, and the American Southwest, is a critical area for future research.

26. Mary Louise Pratt, *Imperial Eyes: Travel Writing and Transculturation* (New York: Routledge, 1992), 5.

27. This critical issue is discussed in chapter 5.

28. Sylvia Rodríguez, *The Matachines Dance: Ritual Symbolism and Interethnic Relations in the Upper Río Grande Valley* (Albuquerque: University of New Mexico Press), 145.

29. This perspective is drawn from the work of Julie Cruikshank, which concentrates on the power of stories in making "meaningful connections." Stories "provide order and continuity in a rapidly changing world." Julie Cruikshank, *The Social Life of Stories: Narrative and Knowledge in the Yukon Territory* (Lincoln: University of Nebraska Press, 1998), xiii.

30. This insight is drawn directly from the work of Robert Sprott ("Making Up What Is Lacking," 18–25), who interprets penitente sacred expression in the history of New Mexico as *kerygma*, or a proclamation, in act and content, of the "death and resurrection of Jesus Christ, the Son of God who gave himself for the sins of humanity (Romans 8:34)." Sprott's focus is on ritual, whereas this work is interested more in belief or myth. The assumption here is that myth (story) is what makes the brotherhood act.

Chapter 5. The Story of Popular Religious Expression in Hispano/Chicano Religions

1. This thesis is identical to the one offered by Jean-Guy A. Goulet in his work on the Dene Tha of Cateh in northwestern Alberta. He defines religion as predominantly experiential. The methodological perspective he offers embraces the thesis that "religious knowledge is derived from personal experiences." Goulet states, "All true knowledge, both knowledge that we would consider mundane and knowledge that we would consider religious, is derived directly from personal experience." Jean-Guy A. Goulet, "Ways of Knowing: Towards a Narrative Ethnography of Experience among the Dene Tha," *Journal of Anthropological Research* 50 (1994): 114.

2. Williams identifies two additional factors that help us identify popular religion in America: The belief and lore of these movements are transmitted through channels other than official seminaries or oral traditions of established religious communities; and popular religious movements generally look for signs of divine intervention or manifestations in the realm of everyday experience, whereas official religion tends to take on characteristics con-

sonant with the broad sociological process called modernization. Peter W. Williams, *Popular Religion in America: Symbolic Change and the Moderniza-tion Process in Historical Development* (Urbana: University of Illinois Press, 1989), 17–18.

3. Samuel Silva Gotay, "The Ideological Dimensions of Popular Religiosity and Cultural Identity in Puerto Rico," in *An Enduring Flame: Studies on Latino Popular Religiosity,* ed. Anthony M. Stevens-Arroyo and Ana María Díaz-Stevens (New York: Bildner Center, 1994), 138.

4. Ibid.

5. Ibid.

6. Orlando O. Espin, "Popular Catholicism among Latinos," in *Hispanic Catholic Culture in the U.S.: Issues and Concerns,* ed. Jay P. Dolan and Allan Figueroa Deck (Notre Dame: University of Notre Dame Press, 1994), 309.

7. Anthony M. Stevens-Arroyo, "Introduction," in *An Enduring Flame: Studies on Latino Popular Religiosity,* ed. Anthony M. Stevens-Arroyo and Ana María Díaz-Stevens (New York: Bildner Center, 1994), 9.

8. Meredith McGuire, "Linking Theory and Methodology for the Study of Latino Religiosity in the United States Context," in *An Enduring Flame: Studies on Latino Popular Religiosity,* ed. Anthony M. Stevens-Arroyo and Ana María Díaz-Stevens (New York: Bildner Center, 1994), 196.

9. The majority of this literature is in the form of doctoral dissertations. The following works are listed in chronological order: Patrick Hayes McNamara, "Bishops, Priests, and Prophecy: A Study in the Sociology of Religious Protest" (University of California, Los Angeles, 1968); Juan Hurtado, "An Attitudinal Study of Social Distance between the Mexican American and the Church" (United States International University, 1976); Sara Marie Murrieta, "The Role of Church Affiliated Hispanic Organization in Meeting Some Significant Needs of Hispanic Americans in the United States" (United States International University, 1977); Gary Charles Rye, "Hispanics and the Roman Catholic Clergy: A Case Study of Conflict" (United States International University, 1977); Antonio Robert Soto, "The Chicano and the Church in Northern California, 1848–1978: A Study of an Ethnic Minority within the Roman Catholic Church" (University of California, Berkeley, 1978); Lawrence J. Mosqueda, *Chicanos, Catholicism and Political Ideology* (Lanham, Md.: University Press of America, 1986); Gilbert Ramón Cadena, "Chicanos and the Catholic Church: Liberation Theology as a Form of Empowerment" (University of California, Riverside, 1987); Alberto L. Pulido, "Race Rela-

tions in the American Catholic Church: An Historical and Sociological Analysis of Mexican American Catholics" (University of Notre Dame, 1989); Jeffrey S. Thies, *Mexican Catholicism in Southern California: The Importance of Popular Religiosity and Sacramental Practice in Faith Experience* (New York: Peter Lang, 1993).

10. David D. Hall, "Introduction," in *Lived Religion in America: Toward a History of Practice,* ed. David D. Hall (Princeton: Princeton University Press, 1997), ix.

11. Richard R. Flores, *Los Pastores: History and Performance in the Mexican Shepherd's Play of South Texas* (Washington, D.C.: Smithsonian Institution Press, 1995), 135.

12. Flores, *Los Pastores,* 143.

13. Ibid.

14. Hall, "Introduction," vii.

15. Robert Anthony Orsi, "Everyday Miracles: The Study of Lived Religion," in *Lived Religion in America: Toward a History of Practice,* ed. David D. Hall (Princeton: Princeton University Press, 1997), 7. Elsewhere, Orsi interprets this place as their "ground of being," which structures a person's actions and reflections within a social-historical context. Robert Anthony Orsi, *The Madonna of 115th Street: Faith and Community in Italian Harlem* (New Haven: Yale University Press, 1985), xvii.

16. C. J. Arthur, "Phenomenology of Religion and the Art of Story-Telling: The Relevance of William Golding's 'The Inheritors' to Religious Studies," *Religious Studies* 23 (1987): 59–79. Also see Pulido, "Mexican American Catholicism," 103.

17. It must be noted that feminist theological scholarship has already begun to tell this story. See in particular Ada María Isasi-Díaz, *En la Lucha: A Hispanic Women's Liberation Theology* (Minneapolis: Fortress Press, 1993); Gloria Inés Loya, "The Hispanic Woman: Pasionaria and Pastora of the Hispanic Community," in *Frontiers of Hispanic Theology in the United States,* ed. Allan Figueroa Deck (Maryknoll: Orbis, 1992).

18. Davíd Carrasco, "Jaguar Christians in the Contact Zone," in *An Enduring Flame: Studies on Latino Popular Religiosity,* ed. Anthony M. Stevens-Arroyo and Ana María Díaz-Stevens (New York: Bildner Center, 1994), 78. In this article, Carrasco argues that these "hidden places" are a significant aspect of Hispano/Chicano religions in the "contact zone," an aspect that scholars must begin to recognize.

Selected Bibliography

Abalos, David T. 1986. *Latinos in the United States*. Notre Dame: University of Notre Dame Press.

———. 1998. *La Comunidad Latina in the United States*. Westport, Conn.: Praeger.

Ahlborn, Richard E. 1986. *The Penitente Moradas of Abiquiú*. Washington, D.C.: Smithsonian Institution Press.

Anaya, Rudolfo A. 1990. "The Writer's Landscape: Epiphany in Landscape." *Latin American Literary Review* 1 (spring): 98–102.

Anaya, Rudolfo A., and Francisco Lomeli, eds. 1993. *Aztlán: Essays in the Chicano Homeland*. Albuquerque: University of New Mexico Press.

Bach, Marcus. 1951. *Faith and My Friends*. Indianapolis: Bobbs-Merrill.

Beck, Warren A. 1982. "The Penitentes of New Mexico." In *Chicano: The Evolution of a People,* ed. Renato Rosaldo, Robert A. Calvert, and Gustav L. Seligmann Jr., 130–38. Malabar, Fla.: Krieger.

Bell, Susan Groag, and Marilyn Yalom, eds. 1990. *Revealing Lives: Autobiography, Biography, and Gender*. Albany: State University of New York Press.

Beshoar, Barron B. 1949. "Western Trails to Calvary." In *Brand Books*. Denver: Westerner.

Briggs, Charles L. 1988. *Competence in Performance: The Creativity of Tradition in Mexicano Verbal Art*. Philadelphia: University of Pennsylvania Press.

Brown, Lorin, Charles L. Briggs, and Marta Weigle. 1978. *Hispano Folklore of New Mexico: The Loin W. Brown Federal Writers Project Manuscripts*. Albuquerque: University of New Mexico.

Bruchac, Joseph. 1996. *Roots of Survival: Native American Storytelling and the Sacred*. Golden, Colo.: Fulcrum.

Bruner, Edward M. 1983. "Introduction: The Opening Up of Anthropology." In *Text, Play, and Story: The Construction and Reconstruction of Self and Society,* ed. Edward M. Bruner. Washington, D.C.: American Ethnological Society.

Buroway, Michael. 1991. *Ethnography Unbound: Power and Resistance in the Modern Metropolis*. Berkeley: University of California Press.

Camarillo, Albert. 1979. *Chicanos in a Changing Society: From Mexican Pueblos to American Barrios in Santa Barbara and Southern California, 1848–1930*. Cambridge: Harvard University Press.

Coca, Benjamin. 1979. *El ermitaño y otras historias religiosas del Norte*. Montezuma, N.M.: Montezuma Publications.

Cruikshank, Julie. 1990. *Life Lived Like a Story*. Lincoln: University of Nebraska Press.

Ciudad Real, Antonio de. 1976. *Relación breve y verdadera de algunas cosas de las muchas que sucedieron al Padre Fray Alonso Ponce*. México: Universidad Nacional Autónoma de México.

Defouri, James H. 1887. *Historical Sketch of the Catholic Church in New Mexico*. San Francisco: McCormick Brothers.

Dundes, Alan, ed. 1984. *Sacred Narrative: Readings in the Theory of Myth*. Berkeley: University of California Press.

Espinosa, Aurelio M. 1985. *The Folklore of Spain in the American Southwest*, ed. J. Manuel Espinosa. Norman: University of Oklahoma.

Fisher, Reginald. 1949. "Notes on the Relations of the Franciscans to the Penitentes." *El Palacio* 43, no. 12 (December 1941): 263–71.

Flynn, Maureen. 1989. *Sacred Charity: Confraternities and Social Welfare in Spain, 1400–1700*. Ithaca: Cornell University Press.

Forrest, Earl R. 1929. *Missions and Pueblos of the Old Southwest*. Cleveland: Arthur H. Clark.

García, Nasario. 1987. *Recuerdos de los viejitos: Tales of the Rio Puerco*. Albuquerque: University of New Mexico Press.

———. 1996. *Comadres: Hispanic Women of the Rio Puerco Valley*. Albuquerque: University of New Mexico Press.

Gorfain, Phyllis, and Edward M. Bruner. 1984. "Dialogic Narration and Paradoxes of Masada." In *Text, Play, and Story: The Construction and Reconstruction of Self and Society*, ed. Edward M. Bruner. Washington, D.C.: American Ethnological Society.

Goss, Linda, and Marian E. Barnes. 1989. *Talk That Talk: An Anthology of African American Storytelling*. New York: Simon and Schuster.

Grimes, Ronald C. 1976. *Symbol and Conquest: Public Ritual and Drama in Santa Fe, New Mexico*. Ithaca: Cornell University Press.

Gutiérrez, Ramón. 1991. *When Jesus Came, the Corn Mother Went Away: Marriage, Sexuality, and Power in New Mexico.* Stanford: Stanford University Press.

Habig, Marion, ed. 1973. *St. Francis of Assisi: Writings and Early Biographies.* Chicago: Franciscan Herald Press.

Halpern, Daniel, ed. 1987. *On Nature: Nature, Landscape, and Natural History.* San Francisco: North Point Press.

Henking, Susan E. 1991. "The Personal Is the Theological: Autobiographical Acts in Contemporary Feminist Theology." *Journal of the Academy of Religion* 59:511–25.

Hobsbawn, Eric, and Terence Ranger, eds. 1983. *The Invention of Tradition.* New York: Cambridge University Press.

Horgan, Paul. 1975. *Lamy of Santa Fe.* New York: Noonday.

How, Louis. 1900. *The Penitentes of San Rafael: A Tale of the San Luis Valley.* New York: Hurst.

Iriate, Lazaro. *Franciscan History: The Three Orders of St. Francis of Assisi.* Chicago: Franciscan Herald Press.

Jaramillo, Cleofas M. 1955. *Romance of a Little Village Girl.* San Antonio: Naylor Company.

Jiménez, Francisco. 1979. *The Identification and Analysis of Chicano Literature.* New York: Bilingual Press.

Johnson, Alonzo, and Paul Jersild, eds. 1996. *"Ain't Gonna Lay My Ligion Down":* *African American Religion in the South.* Columbia: University of Carolina.

Kirkpatrick, Frank G. 1986. *Community: A Trinity of Models.* Washington, D.C.: Georgetown University Press.

Kutz, Jack. 1974. "The Whip and the Cross." *Mankind* 4 (7): 36–40, 60–61.

Lakoff, George, and Mark Johnson. 1980. *Metaphors We Live By.* Chicago: University of Chicago Press.

Lee, Laurence F. 1920. Los Hermanos Penitentes. *El Palacio* 8, no. 1 (January 31): 3–20.

Lummis, Fiske, Turbese Keith Lummis, and Charles F. Lummis. 1975. *The Man and His West.* Norman: University of Oklahoma.

Mitchell, Timothy. 1990. *Passional Culture: Emotion, Religion, and Society in Southern Spain.* Philadelphia: University of Pennsylvania Press.

Orsi, Robert A. 1996. *Thank You, St. Jude: Women's Devotion to the Patron Saint of Hopeless Causes.* New Haven: Yale University Press.

Padget, Martin. 1993. "Cultural Geographies: Travel Writing in the Southwest, 1869–97." Ph.D. diss., University of California, San Diego.

Padilla, Genaro M. 1984. "The Self as Cultural Metaphor in Acosta's Autobiography of a Brown Buffalo." *Journal of General Education* 35 (4): 242–58.

———. 1988. "The Recovery of Chicano Nineteenth-Century Autobiography." *American Quarterly* 40:286–306.

———. 1993. *My History, Not Yours: The Formation of Mexican American Autobiography.* Madison: University of Wisconsin Press.

Paredes, Raymund. 1977. "The Mexican Image in American Travel Literature, 1831–1869." *New Mexico Historical Review* 52, no. 1 (January): 3–29.

Parkhill, Thomas C. 1997. *Weaving Ourselves into the Land.* Albany: State University of New York Press.

Portelli, Alessandro. 1997. *The Battle of Valle Giulia: Oral History and the Art of Dialogue.* Madison: University of Wisconsin Press.

Primo, Leonard Norman. 1993. "Intrinsically Catholic: Vernacular Religion and Philadelphia's 'Dignity.'" Ph.D. diss., University of Pennsylvania.

Prince, L. Bradford. 1977. *Spanish Mission Churches of New Mexico.* Glorieta, N.M.: Rio Grande Press.

Rael, Juan B. 1975. "Arroyo Hondo: Penitentes, Weddings, Wakes." *El Palacio* 81 (1): 4–19.

Randall, Frederika. 1984. "Why Scholars Become Storytellers." *New York Times Book Review* 89 (January 29): 1.

Rebolledo, Tey Diana, ed. 1992. *Nuestras Mujeres: Hispanas of New Mexico, Their Images and Their Lives, 1582–1992.* Albuquerque: El Norte Publications.

Ricard, Robert. 1966. *The Spiritual Conquest of Mexico: An Essay on the Apostolate and the Evangelizing Methods of the Mendicant Orders in New Spain, 1523–1572.* Berkeley: University of California Press.

Rodríguez, Sylvia. 1989. "Art, Tourism, and Race Relations in Taos: Toward a Sociology of the Art Colony." *Journal of Anthropological Research* 45 (1989): 77–99.

Romero, C. Gilbert. 1991. *Hispanic Devotional Piety: Tracing the Biblical Roots.* Maryknoll: Orbis.

Salpointe, J. B. 1967. *Soldiers of the Cross.* Albuquerque: Calvin Horn Publisher.

Segale, Sister Blandina. 1948. *At the End of the Santa Fe Trail.* Milwaukee: Bruce Publishing.

Sommers, Joseph. 1979. "Critical Approaches to Chicano Literature." In *Modern Chicano Writers: A Collection of Critical Essays,* ed. Joseph Sommers and Tomás Ybarra-Frausto, 31–40. Englewood: Prentice Hall.

Steele, Thomas J. 1986. "Cofradía." *The World and I,* August, 149–61.

Steele, Thomas J., Paul Rhetts, and Barbe Awalt. 1998. *Seeds of Struggle, Harvest of Faith: The Papers of the Archdiocese of Santa Fe Catholic Cuarto Centennial Conference of the History of the Catholic Church in New Mexico*. Albuquerque: LPD Press.

Steele, Thomas J., and Rowena A. Rivera. 1985. *Penitente Self-Government: Brotherhoods and Councils, 1797–1947*. Santa Fe: Ancient City Press.

Swatos, William H., ed. 1993. *Future for Religion? New Paradigms for Social Analysis*. Newbury Park, Calif.: Sage.

Thurston, Ann. 1995. *Because of Her Testimony: The Word in Female Experience*. Dublin: Gill and Macmillan.

Underhill, Evelyn. 1968. "St. Francis and Franciscan Spirituality." In *Mixed Pasture: Twelve Essays and Addresses*. Freeport, N.Y.: Books for Libraries Press.

Warner, Louis H. 1936. *Archbishop Lamy: An Epoch Maker*. Santa Fe: Santa Fe New Mexican Publishing.

Weber, David J. 1982. *The Mexican Frontier, 1821–1846: The American Southwest under Mexico*. Albuquerque: University of New Mexico Press.

———. 1992. *The Spanish Frontier in North America*. New Haven: Yale University Press.

Weigle, Martha. 1970. *The Penitentes of the Southwest*. Santa Fe: Ancient City Press.

———, ed. 1983. *Hispanic Arts and Ethnohistory in the Southwest: New Papers Inspired by the Work E. Boyd*. Santa Fe: Ancient City Press.

Weigle, Martha, and Thomas R. Lyons. 1982. "Brothers and Neighbors: The Celebration of Community in Penitente Villages." In *Celebration: Studies in Festivity and Ritual*, ed. Victor Turner, 231–51. Washington, D.C.: Smithsonian Institution Press.

West, John O. 1987. "Grutas at the Crossroads of the Spanish Southwest." *Password* 32 (1): 3–12.

Wiggins, James B. 1975. *Religion as Story*. New York: Harper and Row.

Wilson, Chris. 1997. *The Myth of Santa Fe*. Albuquerque: University of New Mexico Press.

Worster, Donald. 1992. *Under Western Skies: Nature and History in the American West*. New York: Oxford University Press.

Epigraph Sources

Bach, Marcus. 1951. *Faith and My Friends*. Indianapolis: Bobbs-Merrill.

Davis, W. W. H. 1982. *El Gringo: New Mexico and Her People*. Lincoln: University of Nebraska Press.

Gill, Sam D. 1987. *Mother Earth: An American Story.* Chicago: University of Chicago Press.

Hongo, Garrett. 1995. *Under Western Eyes: Personal Essays from Asian America.* New York: Anchor Books.

Kutsche, Paul, and Dennis Gallegos. 1979. "Community Functions of the Confradía de Nuestro Padre Jesús Nazareno." In *The Colorado Studies: The Survival of the Spanish American Villages.* No. 15 (Spring 1979): 91–98.

Powell, E. Alexander. 1926. *In Barbary; Tunisia, Algeria, Morocco, and the Sahara.* New York and London: The Century Co.

Sánchez-Carcía, Taida. 1992. "Yo sé que viví muy a gusto/I Know I Lived Very Comfortably." In *Abuelitos: Stories of the Río Puerco Valley,* ed. Nasario García. Albuquerque: University of New Mexico Press.

Wideman, John Edgar. 1994. *Fatheralong: A Meditation on Fathers and Sons, Race and Society.* New York: Pantheon Books.

Index